The Creative Curriculum® for Infants, Toddlers & Twos
Second Edition, Revised

Volume 1: The Foundation

Diane Trister Dodge
Sherrie Rudick
Kai-leé Berke

Contributing Authors: Donna Bloomer, Laura J. Colker,
Amy Laura Dombro, and Diane Woodard

TeachingStrategies® · Washington, D.C.

Copyright © 2011 by Teaching Strategies, Inc.

All rights reserved. No part of this text may be reproduced in any form or by any electronic or mechanical means, including information storage and retrieval systems, without prior written permission from Teaching Strategies, Inc., except in the case of brief quotations embodied in critical articles or reviews.

An exception is also made for the forms that are included in this volume. Permission is granted to duplicate those pages for use by the teachers and care providers of the particular program that purchased *The Creative Curriculum® for Infants, Toddlers & Twos* in order to implement the curriculum in the program. However, the material on those pages may not be duplicated for training purposes without the express written permission of Teaching Strategies, Inc.

The publisher and the authors cannot be held responsible for injury, mishap, or damages incurred during the use of or because of the information in this book. The authors recommend appropriate and reasonable supervision at all times based on the age and capability of each child.

Editors: Toni Bickart and Laurie Taub
Cover design: Abner Nieves
Interior illustrations: Jennifer Barrett O'Connell
Layout/production: Jeff Cross

The drawing of toys, equipment, and furniture on page 66 is based on products offered by Community Playthings.

The drawing of toys and equipment on page 24 is based on products offered by Kaplan Early Learning Company.

Teaching Strategies, Inc.
P.O. Box 42243
Washington, DC 20015
www.TeachingStrategies.com
ISBN: 978-1-60617-415-9

Teaching Strategies and *The Creative Curriculum* names and logos are registered trademarks of Teaching Strategies, Inc., Washington, D.C. Brand-name products of other companies are suggested for illustrative purposes and are not required for implementation of the curriculum.

Library of Congress Cataloging-in-Publication Data

Dodge, Diane Trister.
  The creative curriculum for infants, toddlers & twos / Diane Trister Dodge, Sherrie Rudick, Kai-leé Berke ; Donna Bloomer ... [et al.], contributing authors. -- 2nd ed., rev.
     p. cm.
  ISBN 978-1-60617-415-9 (v. 1) -- ISBN 978-1-60617-416-6 (v. 2) -- ISBN 978-1-60617-417-3 (v. 3)
  1. Education, Preschool--Curricula--United States. 2. Child care--United States. 3. Curriculum planning--United States. 4. Child development--United States. I. Rudick, Sherrie. II. Berke, Kai-leé. III. Title.

LB1140.4.D632 2011
372.19--dc22
                        2010038683

Printed and bound in the United States of America
2015   2014   2013   2012   2011
10 9 8 7 6 5 4 3 2

Acknowledgments

More than 10 years ago, my colleagues and I ventured into developing a curriculum for programs serving children from birth to age 3. We shared the field's increasing recognition that this period of development is vital. We were also responding to many requests from those who work with families to provide care and education for our youngest children. They were seeking guidance about offering appropriate and rich programs. My co-authors and I are deeply grateful to the dedicated and caring early childhood educators who continue to inform our work by generously sharing their challenges and experiences and letting us know what they need to help them plan and implement high-quality programs.

This revised edition of *The Creative Curriculum® for Infants, Toddlers & Twos* includes content developed with Amy Dombro and Laura Colker, my co-authors of the first edition. They taught me much about infant–toddler programs and enthusiastically joined the adventure of developing one of the first curricula for this age-group. Along with many other colleagues and practitioners, Amy and Laura provided input when the second edition was developed. Our appreciation also goes to Tess Bennett, Carol Gestwicki, Janice Im, Gail Kelso, Jean Monroe, Sherry Nolte, Jerry Parr, Miriam L. Perreira, Sarah Semlak, and Kim Thuerauf. Special thanks go to Monica Vacca for her guidance on children with disabilities, Betsy Shelby-Morris for her suggestions on sharing stories and books with children with disabilities, and Dawn Terrill for her contributions to the discussions of dual-language learning.

Our 38 new objectives for children's development and learning are a major reason for revising *The Creative Curriculum® for Infants, Toddlers & Twos. Volume 3: Objectives for Development & Learning* is an essential resource for all educators who base their programs on knowledge of child development and what they learn about each child in their care. My deep appreciation goes to the many colleagues who worked tirelessly for over 4 years to develop this essential addition to the curriculum. The objectives are also the focus of *Teaching Strategies GOLD*™, our new, seamless system for ongoing, observation-based assessment. While *Teaching Strategies GOLD*™ can be used with any developmentally appropriate curriculum, it is linked directly with all Teaching Strategies resources.

Special thanks go to Toni Bickart and Laurie Taub for their thoughtful and detailed editing. Jennifer Barrett O'Connell, our illustrator, brought the children and teachers to life and provided a vision of what we hoped to convey through our words. We thank our design and production team for the layout of this revised edition: Julie Sebastianelli, Margot Ziperman, Jeff Cross, and Abner Nieves.

Diane Trister Dodge

Contents

Volume 1: The Foundation

Introduction xi
    What a Comprehensive Curriculum Offers   xi
    Essential Aspects of Responsive Care   xii
    How This Edition Is Organized   xii
    Getting Started   xv

Theory and Research 1
    Meeting Children's Basic Needs 2
    Abraham Maslow   2
    T. Berry Brazelton and Stanley Greenspan   2

    Fostering Social–Emotional Development 4
    Erik Erikson   4
    Stanley Greenspan   5

    Developing Relationships 7
    Attachment   7
    Resilience   8

    Supporting Cognition and Brain Development 10
    Jean Piaget   10
    Lev Vygotsky   12
    Brain Research   13

Chapter 1: Knowing Infants, Toddlers, and Twos 16
    What Infants, Toddlers, and Twos Are Like 18
    Social–Emotional Development   18
    Physical Development   21
    Language Development   24
    Cognitive Development   27

    Individual Differences 30
    Temperament   30
    Life Circumstances   33
    Dual-Language Learners   34
    Disabilities   35

Contents

Chapter 2: Creating a Responsive Environment.....38

Setting Up the Physical Environment.....40
Creating Places for Routines and Experiences   41
Designing Spaces for Each Age-Group   43
Selecting Materials   50
Displaying Materials   52
Special Considerations in Setting Up the Physical Environment   53
Sending Positive Messages   58

Creating a Structure for Each Day.....61
Planning a Daily Schedule   61
Individualizing the Schedule for Infants   62
Schedules for Toddlers and Twos   66
Planning for Transitions   69
Responsive Planning   70

Chapter 3: What Children Are Learning.....78

The Foundation for All Learning.....80

Building Language and Literacy Skills.....81
Vocabulary and Language   81
The Sounds and Rhythms of Language   83
Enjoying Books and Stories   85
Exploring Writing   87
Promoting Language and Literacy Learning   89

Discovering Mathematical Relationships.....92
Number Concepts   92
Patterns and Relationships   93
Geometry and Spatial Relationships   94
Sorting and Classifying   95
Helping Children Discover Mathematical Relationships   96

Exploring Like Scientists.....98
The Physical World   98
The Natural World   99
The Social World   100
Encouraging Children to Explore Like Scientists   101

Chapter 4: Caring and Teaching 104

Building Relationships 106
Strategies for Building Trusting Relationships 106
Helping Children Get Along With Others 108
A Structure That Supports Relationships 110
Helping Children Transition to a New Group or Preschool 112

Promoting Children's Self-Regulation 113
Setting the Foundation for Young Infants' Self-Regulation 113
Helping Mobile Infants Begin to Control Their Behavior 114
Promoting the Self-Regulation of Toddlers and Twos 114
Using Positive Guidance Strategies 116

Responding to Challenging Behaviors 119
Physical Aggression 119
Temper Tantrums 120
Biting 121

Guiding Children's Learning 124
Learning Through Play 125
Talking With Infants, Toddlers, and Twos 127
Extending Children's Knowledge and Skills 128
Including All Children 129

Assessing Children's Development and Learning 132
Step 1: Observing and Collecting Facts 132
Step 2: Analyzing and Responding 136
Step 3: Evaluating Each Child's Progress 137
Step 4: Summarizing, Planning, and Communicating 138

Chapter 5: Building Partnerships With Families ... 140

Special Concerns of Families With Children Under Age 3 ... 142
The Stress of Parenting an Infant — 142
Conflicting Feelings About Sharing Care — 143
Wanting to Be Part of Their Child's Day — 143

Getting to Know Families ... 144
Appreciating Differences Among Families — 144
Understanding the Influence of Culture — 145

Welcoming Families to Your Program ... 146
Creating a Welcoming Environment — 146
Orienting New Families — 147
Developing an Individual Care Plan for Each Child — 148
Reaching Out to All Family Members — 149

Communicating With Families ... 150
Building Trust Through Daily Interactions — 150
Making the Most of Daily Exchanges — 152
Communicating in More Formal Ways — 154
Holding Conferences With Families — 155
Making Home Visits — 157

Involving Families in the Program ... 158
Offering a Variety of Ways to Be Involved — 158
Participating in the Program — 160

Sharing Information and Parenting Tips ... 161

Responding to Challenging Situations ... 162
Resolving Differences: A Partnership Approach — 162
Working Through Conflicts — 165
Supporting Families Who Are Under Stress — 169
Supporting the Families of Children With Disabilities — 171

Appendix..175

    Individual Care Plan—Family Information Form   176
    Individual Care Plan   179
    Child Planning Form   180
    Group Planning Form   181
    Family Conference Form   182

References..183

General Resources...185

Volume 2: Routines and Experiences 187–385

Volume 3: Objectives for Development & Learning 1–206

Introduction

The care that infants, toddlers, and twos receive and their experiences during the first 3 years of life have a powerful influence on the way they view the world, relate to others, and succeed as learners. As a teacher, you have a unique opportunity to make a difference in the lives of very young children and their families.

Birth to age 3 is the most important period of development and a period in which children are very vulnerable. Initially, they are totally dependent on adults to meet their every need. When their care and experiences are nurturing, consistent, and loving, children flourish. Almost every day you can see exciting changes as children learn to trust you, joyfully explore the environment you have created, make discoveries, care about others, and begin to see themselves as competent learners. Infants, toddlers, and twos who receive high-quality care are more likely to become sociable, capable preschoolers who get along with others, develop self-control, and love learning.

Your influence on children and families depends on the quality of the program you provide. Organizations like ZERO TO THREE and the National Association for the Education of Young Children have identified the factors that define a high-quality program for infants, toddlers, and twos. Caring for children under age 3 is too important to leave to chance. Teachers must be intentional about what they do each day in their work with children and families. That is why we offer this comprehensive, developmentally appropriate curriculum.

What a Comprehensive Curriculum Offers

A curriculum is like a road map; it helps you get where you want to go. A comprehensive, developmentally appropriate curriculum, such as *The Creative Curriculum® for Infants, Toddlers & Twos*, includes objectives for children's development and learning. Objectives define where you want to go, and the curriculum tells you how to get there. Curriculum is the what, why, how, and when of providing a high-quality program. It also guides the interactions you have with children and families. *The Creative Curriculum®* explains all aspects of a developmentally appropriate program and leads you through the processes of planning and offering excellent care and education for infants, toddlers, and twos.

Just as a road map gives you choices about what routes to take, *The Creative Curriculum®* offers choices and encourages flexibility. What makes caring for infants, toddlers, and twos so enjoyable and satisfying is your ability to appreciate the everyday discoveries that delight a child: the colors dancing on the wall as light passes through a prism, the jingling bells in a toy, the amazing accomplishment of a first step, finally fitting a puzzle piece into place. *The Creative Curriculum®* helps you be intentional about the experiences you offer infants, toddlers, and twos while still having the flexibility to respond to the changing interests and abilities of the young children in your care.

Essential Aspects of Responsive Care

The three volumes of *The Creative Curriculum® for Infants, Toddlers & Twos* discuss many aspects of providing responsive care for very young children:

- Building a trusting relationship with each child
- Providing individualized care
- Creating environments that support and encourage exploration
- Ensuring children's safety and health
- Developing partnerships with families
- Observing and documenting children's development in order to plan for each child and the group
- Recognizing the importance of social–emotional development
- Appreciating cultural, family, and individual differences
- Taking advantage of every opportunity to build a foundation for lifelong learning
- Supporting dual-language learners
- Including children with disabilities in all aspects of the program

How This Edition Is Organized

This revised edition of *The Creative Curriculum® for Infants, Toddlers & Twos* includes three volumes. The first two are updated editions. Our new objectives for the development and learning of children from birth through kindergarten were a major reason for revising them. The 38 objectives are explained in great detail in the third volume and referred to frequently throughout the first two volumes.

The Creative Curriculum® for Infants, Toddlers & Twos Volume 1: The Foundation

The first volume begins with an overview of the theory and research that underlie the curriculum's focus on meeting children's basic needs, fostering secure attachments and promoting other aspects of social–emotional development, helping children develop secure attachments, and supporting cognition and brain development. *Volume 1* has five chapters, each of which presents one of the central components that together give you the information you need to set up your program and work effectively with children and families.

The figure on the right shows how these five components form a framework that teachers apply during each of the routines and learning experiences.

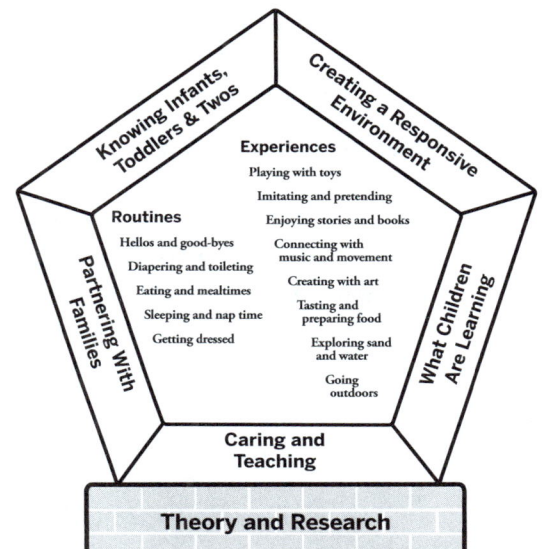

Chapter 1, Knowing Infants, Toddlers, and Twos explains the social–emotional, physical, cognitive, and language development of children and lists the curricular objectives for each area. It also discusses the characteristics that make each child unique, including temperament, life experiences, dual-language learning, and the presence of a disability.

Chapter 2, Creating a Responsive Environment offers a model for setting up the physical environment for routines and experiences in ways that address the developing abilities and interests of infants, toddlers, and twos. It shows how to create a daily schedule and weekly plans that give you direction but allow flexibility.

Chapter 3, What Children Are Learning shows how the responsive relationship you form with each child, the interactions you have every day, and the materials and experiences you offer become the building blocks for successful learning. Language and literacy, discovering mathematical relationships, and scientific explorations are part of this discussion. Art and music and movement are addressed in later chapters.

Chapter 4, Caring and Teaching describes the varied and interrelated roles of teachers who work with infants, toddlers, and twos. It offers strategies for building positive relationships, helping children develop self-regulation, and responding to challenging behaviors. It shows how to guide children's learning during daily routines and everyday experiences. Finally, it explains the role of ongoing assessment in learning about each child, following children's progress, and planning.

Chapter 5, Building Partnerships With Families explores the benefits of working with families as partners in the care of their children. It explains how partnerships are built by exchanging information on a daily basis, involving families in all aspects of the program, communicating in respectful ways, and working through differences in ways that sustain the partnership and benefit the child.

The Creative Curriculum® for Infants, Toddlers & Twos Volume 2: Routines and Experiences

The second volume includes chapters on each of the daily routines and experiences that make up a child's day. It has two parts.

Part A: Routines (chapters 6–10) shows how daily routines are an important part of the curriculum and important times to put research and theory into practice. Routines are opportunities to build positive relationships with children and promote trust. The one-on-one time you spend easing children and families through hellos and good-byes, diapering and toileting, feeding, dressing, and soothing children to sleep helps infants, toddlers, and twos learn to feel secure with you. As they gain new skills and participate more actively in daily routines, they develop a sense of their own competence. Routines are also times to nurture children's curiosity and guide them as they make increasing sense of their world.

Part B: Experiences (chapters 11–18) offers guidance about appropriate materials and interactions. It discusses ways to engage children in playing with toys, imitating and pretending, enjoying stories and books, connecting with music and movement, creating with art, tasting and preparing food, exploring sand and water, and going outdoors. This section also explains that, while planning for these experiences is important, you are only *planning for possibilities* because you must be able to respond to whatever interests a child.

The Creative Curriculum® for Infants, Toddlers & Twos Volume 3: Objectives for Development & Learning: Birth Through Kindergarten

The third volume provides detailed information about each of the 38 objectives for children's development and learning. These are the same objectives as those of the *Teaching Strategies GOLD™ assessment system,* a powerful tool for observing children, documenting their changing abilities, and individualizing your interactions with each child. Using ongoing assessment to decide how to respond to each child and to plan appropriate experiences enables you to care for and teach all children effectively.

Whether or not you use the *Teaching Strategies GOLD™* assessment system, it is important for you to be familiar with the objectives for development and learning. The objectives identify the behaviors, skills and knowledge that are most predictive of school success. While school is a few years away for infants, toddlers, and twos, the foundation for future development and learning is established in these very important early years. *Volume 3: Objectives for Development & Learning* presents the research related to each objective, explains why each objective is important, shows the developmental progression for each objective, and includes strategies to support children's development and learning as it relates to each objective.

The first 36 objectives are organized into nine areas of development and learning:

Social–Emotional	Mathematics
Physical	Science and Technology
Language	Social Studies
Cognitive	The Arts
Literacy	

A tenth area, English Language Acquisition, applies to children who are learning to understand and express themselves in English while they are also learning the language(s) spoken in their homes.

Not all objectives apply to children from birth. We use a color-coded system to show you when children typically begin demonstrating the behaviors, skills, and knowledge related to each objective.

Getting Started

You may not have used a curriculum or assessment system in your work with infants, toddlers, and twos before. You do not have to read the entire book or learn the entire assessment process before beginning to use these resources. Find the topics that are of most importance to your work and start with those chapters. You will find a lot of information that immediately supports your daily work, especially your interactions with children and families. We explain how to plan and provide responsive care for children in four age-groups. The ages overlap a bit because children develop according to individual timetables and because programs define age-groups in a number of ways. These are the four groups in *The Creative Curriculum® for Infants, Toddlers & Twos*:

- young infants (0–9 months)
- mobile infants (8–18 months)
- toddlers (16–25 months)
- twos (24–36 months)

In every chapter, we give examples of what children do at different ages and how teachers provide responsive care. For each age-group, we have imagined several children and their teachers. They are introduced here.

Julio, 4 months, with his teacher, Linda

Jasmine, 8 months, with her teacher, Janet

Willard, 11 months, with his teacher, Grace

Abby, 14 months, with her teacher, Brooks

Introduction

Leo, 18 months, with his teacher, Barbara

Matthew, 22 months, with his teacher, Mercedes

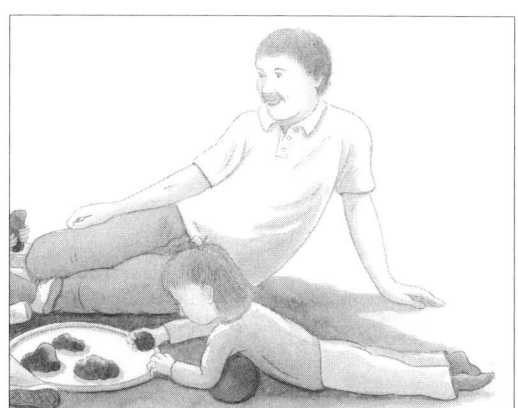

Gena, 30 months, with her teacher, Ivan

Valisha and Jonisha, 33-month-old twins, with their teacher, LaToya

Theory and Research

Until the 20th century, scientific researchers gave little attention to children's development and learning. In the past 75 years, however, research has generated new information about childhood as a separate and distinct stage of life. Developmentally appropriate practice is the application of this knowledge to teaching. *The Creative Curriculum® for Infants, Toddlers & Twos* shows you how to implement developmentally appropriate practice in your program for young children.

Developmentally appropriate practice means teaching in ways that match the way children develop and learn. According to the National Association for the Education of Young Children, quality care requires that early childhood professionals make decisions about the care and education of children based upon information in three areas:[1]

- knowledge of child development and how children learn
- knowledge of the individual needs, strengths, and interests of each child
- knowledge of the social and cultural context in which each child lives

This section summarizes some of the major theories behind developmentally appropriate practice and *The Creative Curriculum®*. Each of the theories or research described has influenced the design of *The Creative Curriculum®* and its view of how children develop and learn. The chapter also explains how *The Creative Curriculum®* helps you put theory and research into practice in your program. It will help you decide what to do when, for example, an infant cries for the first several days in your care. It will help you understand such things as why a mobile infant pushes her toys one by one off the table, watching them fall. You will know what to do when a toddler shouts, "No!" when you ask him to do something. Understanding early childhood theory and research is essential to knowing what children think and feel and how you can help them become caring people and joyful learners.

Meeting Children's Basic Needs

All people have basic needs. Abraham Maslow, a 20th century psychologist, suggested that people's basic needs must be met before higher-level learning can take place. Respected child development experts Stanley Greenspan and T. Berry Brazelton focused on the particular needs of children. They have taken a broader, more comprehensive approach to addressing children's needs.

Abraham Maslow

Abraham Maslow described a hierarchy of needs common to all human beings.[2] Needs that involve physiology, safety, belonging, and esteem are extremely important in the care of very young children. Physiological needs are hunger, thirst, and bodily comfort. Knowing that a hungry child has difficulty focusing on relationships and learning, many early childhood programs provide breakfast, snacks, and lunch, and they feed each infant according to his or her own schedule. Safety involves security and freedom from danger. When children feel protected and believe that no harm will come to them, they are better able to interact with others and to explore their environment. Belonging is the sense of being comfortable with and connected to others. Feeling connected depends upon being accepted, respected, and loved. Esteem involves self-respect and respect from others. Esteem emerges from daily experiences that give children the opportunity to discover that they are capable learners.

More recent reviewers of Maslow's theory have argued that meeting people's needs in a particular order is not always necessary, and basic needs are not as simplistic as Maslow's hierarchy suggests. However, his research did demonstrate that certain basic needs must be met in order for children to benefit from the experiences you offer.

T. Berry Brazelton and Stanley Greenspan

T. Berry Brazelton and Stanley Greenspan described children's specific needs in their book, *The Irreducible Needs of Children*.[3] They explained that children need

- ongoing, nurturing relationships
- physical protection, safety, and regulation
- experiences tailored to their individual differences
- developmentally appropriate experiences
- limit setting, structure, and expectations
- stable, supportive communities and cultural continuity
- adults to protect their future

These seven needs expand upon Maslow's basic needs. They underlie the principles of developmentally appropriate practice, particularly the important role that families, teachers, and communities play in children's lives. When parents, teachers, and communities meet all seven of these needs, children are prepared socially, emotionally, and intellectually for future life success.

In *The Creative Curriculum®*, your ability to meet children's needs is essential to providing responsive care and education. Children are able to learn and grow when they feel safe and cared for, are appropriately challenged and guided, and have strong relationships with nurturing adults.

> **Valisha** (33 months) is busy adding animals to her block building when LaToya announces that it is clean-up time. Jonisha (33 months) says, "You gotta clean up now, Valisha." Valisha looks at her angrily and says, "No!" as she reaches to push Jonisha away. LaToya immediately intervenes, knowing that she must make sure that the children in her care are safe. She says, "Valisha, be safe. I will not let you push your sister." By saying this, LaToya intentionally and clearly limits Valisha's behavior.
>
> To show Valisha that she respects her feelings, LaToya adds, "It sounds as though you are frustrated because you don't want to clean up your building." When Valisha says, "I'm making a house for my animals. I don't wanna go outside," LaToya considers what to say. She wants to honor Valisha's feelings and preference while clarifying expectations for group behavior. "Valisha, I have to go outside with the other children now. It isn't safe for you to be inside by yourself. Would you like to put a Please save sign on your building so that no one puts it away? Then you can come back and play with it when we come inside again." Valisha nods her head, "Yes."

Major Ideas	*The Creative Curriculum®*
Abraham Maslow Needs that involve physiology, safety, belonging, and esteem must be met in order for children to be able to build relationships and learn.	• Create an environment in which children are safe, feel emotionally secure, and have a sense of belonging. • Provide responsive caregiving that meets children's individual needs.
T. Berry Brazelton and Stanley Greenspan Seven needs must be met in order for children to develop and learn. They underlie the principles of developmentally appropriate practice, particularly the important role that families, teachers, and communities play in children's lives.	• Establish and maintain nurturing relationships with children. • Provide safe, developmentally appropriate learning experiences. • Individualize schedules, routines, and experiences to meet each child's needs. • Create partnerships with families to support children's development and learning. • Set limits and guide learning in ways that reflect realistic expectations for children's behavior.

Fostering Social–Emotional Development

The positive social–emotional development of infants, toddlers, and twos is nurtured when they develop trusting relationships with the important adults in their lives. As trust develops, they begin to see themselves as separate, capable human beings who can understand and control their emotions.

Erik Erikson

Erik Erikson's theory of the "Eight Stages of Man" identifies a sequence of main psychological tasks that need to be resolved for healthy development to occur.[4] According to Erikson, each stage builds on successfully resolving the conflict of earlier stages. During the first 3 years, children are challenged by the conflicts of trust versus mistrust (infancy) and autonomy versus shame and doubt (ages 1–3). For each stage, Erikson describes what adults need to provide in order to help children meet the challenges facing them.

According to Erikson, **trust** develops when your experiences show you that the world around you is safe, reliable, and responsive to your needs. Infants who receive consistent and loving care learn to trust themselves, others, and the world around them. They are then free to explore their environment and have the foundation for developing positive relationships with others. Infants develop mistrust when they cry but get no response, are not fed when they are hungry, or are not comforted when they are hurt. They learn that they cannot count on adults to meet their needs, and they mistrust their own ability to affect the world around them. Maintaining a reliable, safe, and comforting atmosphere reinforces the trust children learn at home and helps children who may mistrust because of difficult experiences.

Autonomy, or independence, requires a sense of one's own power. It is built on the foundation of trust described in Erikson's first stage of development. Children develop autonomy when adults give them opportunities to do things successfully on their own. When adults make too many demands or criticize children's efforts, children develop shame and doubt. You help children become autonomous by honoring their efforts and providing experiences that foster their sense of competence. You also set clear limits so toddlers feel safe to explore their newfound independence.

Your most important role is to establish trusting relationships with the children in your care. When children learn that they can trust you, they are open to exploring the world around them, and they will be able to develop autonomy.

Stanley Greenspan

In a separate body of work, Stanley Greenspan charted six milestones in young children's emotional growth.[5] Like Erikson, Greenspan believed that children need supportive, trusting relationships with the important adults in their lives. He explained that, when children have such relationships as their foundation, they grow socially, emotionally, and cognitively. The milestones mark the emotional development of children from birth through age 4.

Milestone 1: Self-regulation and interest in the world—During this first stage, young infants have their own ways of dealing with sensations, taking in and acting on information, and finding ways to calm and soothe themselves. They need you and their parents to take note of these individual differences and respond to them accordingly. *The Creative Curriculum*® guides you to learn and appreciate each child's unique ways of being and to respond to them appropriately.

Milestone 2: Falling in love (relating to others in a warm, trusting manner)—Mastery of this milestone means that a baby has learned that relationships can be joyful and that warmth and love are possible. That is why your major responsibility is to establish trusting, nurturing relationships with the children in your care. Important motor, cognitive, and language skills also develop that help the baby establish relationships with primary caregivers. By 5 months, some infants eagerly reach out for relationships. They return your smiles, watch your face with great interest, and relax when held. Others may be more hesitant to establish relationships. These infants need you and their parents to continue to reach out to them, even when they ignore or reject some of your attempts to engage them.

Milestone 3: Developing intentional, two-way communication—By this stage, infants need to know that their families and teachers will understand and respond appropriately to the signals they use to communicate. For example, they need adults to interpret the cues that signal their need for calm or their readiness to play. *The Creative Curriculum*® places a high priority on responding appropriately to children's communication attempts. When you do this, you reinforce their intentional expression of needs and wants through gestures, facial expressions, and vocalizations.

Milestone 4: Emergence of an organized sense of self and problem-solving ability— Infants, toddlers, and twos need adults to recognize and appreciate their ability to assert themselves and their new abilities. *The Creative Curriculum*® encourages you to follow a child's lead during play, extend her play, and help her shift from one experience to another. By doing this, you help her see herself as an individual. *The Creative Curriculum*® also shows you how to enforce appropriate limits, offer her opportunities to explore, respond to her requests, and help her solve problems.

Milestone 5: Creating emotional ideas—During this stage, children use pretend play to explore their feelings and make sense of their world. When you help children express their feelings through words and gestures, you promote their emotional development. If children's emotions make you uncomfortable, you may find yourself stopping play that includes anger and aggression. Rather than limiting children's exploration of these emotions, *The Creative Curriculum*® encourages you to acknowledge their feelings and model or suggest an appropriate way to express them.

Milestone 6: Emotional thinking—By this milestone, children link ideas and begin to deal with the world logically. For example, rather than simply hugging a doll, a child might explain that the doll is sad because she fell down and hurt her knee. They begin to connect ideas that pertain to "me" and "not me" and to distinguish reality from fantasy. *The Creative Curriculum®* explains how to help toddlers and twos connect their ideas by asking them about their opinions and by extending their play. You also help them realize that actions have consequences and that the present has implications for the future.

Major Ideas	*The Creative Curriculum®*
Erik Erikson Social and emotional learning is a lifelong process that begins at birth. When adults are responsive to children's needs, children resolve the tension between trust and mistrust, and between autonomy and shame.	• Develop and maintain a trusting relationship with each child. • Implement nurturing, trust-building routines. • Provide responsive caregiving to meet the individual needs of children. • Provide learning experiences that help children feel competent. • Offer children appropriate choices and challenges.
Stanley Greenspan Six emotional milestones mark the emotional development of very young children. Children develop an understanding of themselves and the world through relationships and emotions.	• Assign primary caregivers to infants and toddlers, to help build trusting, loving relationships. • Talk with children, even before they understand anything you are saying. • Respond to children's attempts to communicate. • Help children express their emotions appropriately. • Provide many opportunities for pretend play.

Developing Relationships

Research about attachment and resilience provides guidance about other aspects of social–emotional development of infants, toddlers, and twos. It confirms the importance of the development of trusting relationships with the important adults in their lives.

Attachment

Attachment theory describes the processes through which people form close relationships with others. **John Bowlby's** research recognized that infants become attached to the important people in their lives.[6] On the basis of their deep emotional bonds, young children learn about their self-worth, relationships with others, and which emotions should be expressed and how. Their first relationships create the foundation for future relationships with others.

When children's needs are consistently met in a nurturing, responsive way by a trusted adult and when they have many positive interactions with that adult, children learn that they are important and that they can count on others. However, not all attachments are based on trusting, loving relationships. **Mary Ainsworth's** research on attachment demonstrated that there are two primary types: secure and insecure. Each has a different effect on how infants and toddlers behave, develop, and learn.[7]

Secure attachments develop when infants are cared for by adults who meet their needs consistently, accurately, and lovingly. These infants know that they can rely on the important people in their lives to meet their basic needs, to provide comfort when they are upset, and to share the joy of their everyday interactions. Consistent, nurturing care teaches children that they are important and helps them develop a positive sense of self. Children who develop secure attachments to one or more adults are more likely to develop positive social skills. They gradually acquire an understanding of their emotions and the emotions of others because of their interactions with nurturing caregivers.

Insecure attachments develop when adults are unpredictable, insensitive, uninformed, unresponsive, or threatening. A mother who pays attention to her child only when she wants, rather than when the baby needs her to, is being insensitive and unpredictable. A teacher who sometimes responds lovingly when the baby cries but who generally does not respond at all is being unresponsive. Children also develop insecure attachments when their caregivers are threatening, such as when they respond angrily to a baby's crying or when they physically or emotionally abuse the baby or other members of the household. Insecure attachments can make children feel badly about themselves, lack self-control, and struggle to develop positive relationships with others.

These two types of attachment reflect the quality of the relationship between the adult and the child; they are not determined by the child, himself. *The Creative Curriculum*® supports and encourages secure attachments between you and the children in your care.

> **Grace** and her co-teacher each have three babies for whom they are primarily responsible. Every day during Willard's (11 months) first week in Grace's care, he cried most of the time. Grace held Willard close to her body for periods of time, using a baby carrier that his family offered. This allowed her to have her hands free while still being responsive to Willard's need for physical closeness. Grace also used diaper changing, meals, and naps as key times during the day to talk with Willard, reassure him that she would meet his needs, and respond empathetically to his crying.
>
> During the beginning of the second week, as Willard began to understand that he could count on Grace to be a consistent, loving presence for him, he was able to relax. He cried less frequently and began to explore his exciting new environment.

Resilience

The ability to recover from stress or to manage the effects of a difficult situation and function effectively is called *resilience*. The research on resilience, which began in the 1970s, has focused on children who develop well despite hardships. Perhaps the most significant result of this work has been to challenge the assumption that children growing up under the threat of disadvantage and hardship are doomed to a life of problems. Research has shown that children can develop the strength and skills necessary to deal positively with adversity.[8]

This research has also begun to provide information about the kind of help that children threatened by harmful conditions need in order to thrive. Not surprisingly, the research consistently notes the importance of teachers.

The basic foundation of resilience is developed when very young children

- form close, trusting relationships with the important adults in their lives
- have adults who help them understand their feelings and the feelings of others
- receive the necessary adult support to develop self-control
- have opportunities to develop a sense of their own competence

These findings inform the core belief that underlies *The Creative Curriculum*®: It is essential for teachers to develop a positive, nurturing, supportive relationship with each child. As young children develop language, responsive adults help them learn about themselves and others and the need to learn self-control. Their positive relationships with caring adults help children develop social–emotional skills and a positive self image. The strategies that *The Creative Curriculum*® presents encourage these foundations of resiliency and enable teachers to help children develop and learn, even though they cannot change the difficult circumstances in which some families live.

> **Julio** (4 months) wakes from his nap and begins to cry. Knowing that it is extremely important for him to trust her, Linda immediately lifts him out of his crib. She gently pats his back, trying to soothe him. Over time, as he learns that he can rely on her, this trusting relationship helps him develop resilience.
>
> Holding him, she realizes that he has a wet diaper. Linda knows that talking with Julio about his discomfort will eventually help him understand his emotions. As they walk to the diaper changing table, she says, "Oh, sweet bebé. You are sad because your diaper is wet. Let's go put on a dry one."

Major Ideas | *The Creative Curriculum*®

Major Ideas	*The Creative Curriculum*®
Attachment When children's needs are met consistently in a nurturing way by a trusted adult and when they have many positive interactions with that adult, children learn that they are important and that they can count on others. When they develop a secure attachment with one or more caregivers, children feel more confident about exploring the world around them and developing relationships with others.	• Assign a primary teacher to each child. • Provide responsive, loving care that meets the individual needs of children. • Use nurturing routines (diaper changing, eating and mealtime, hellos and good-byes, sleeping, and getting dressed) to develop and maintain a trusting relationship with each child. • Respond appropriately to children's communication attempts. Provide responsive caregiving to meet the individual needs of children.
Resilience When young children develop close, trusting relationships with the important adults in their lives, the most basic foundation for the further development of resiliency is laid.	• Develop and maintain a trusting relationship with each child. • Teach language for the expression of feelings. • Offer appropriate levels of support to help children develop self-control. • Provide opportunities for children to practice their new skills.

Supporting Cognition and Brain Development

Infants, toddlers, and twos develop cognitively when they have many opportunities to explore the world around them, interact with others, and play. The work of Jean Piaget and Lev Vygotsky, as well as recent brain research, provide a deeper understanding of why these experiences are so important for young children. Research findings also help us determine what teachers and families can do to support cognitive development.

Jean Piaget

Jean Piaget was interested in the way logical thinking develops.[9] Like Erikson and Greenspan, Piaget described development as a progression through stages. He showed that infants think differently from young children, that young children think differently from older children, and that older children think differently from adults.

Piaget thought that children refine their logic and construct understandings about the world through play. By handling materials of different sizes, shapes, and colors, children eventually learn to sort, classify, compare, and sequence. Their knowledge grows as they experiment, make discoveries, and modify their earlier way of thinking to incorporate new insights. Piaget called the processes *accommodation* and *assimilation*.

Accommodation occurs when a child's experience does not fit his previous understanding. He must change his thinking about the subject in order for it to make sense again. For example, imagine a toddler who lives in a house with several small dogs and who believes all dogs are small. When she sees a big animal that barks and her father tells her that it is a dog, she has to change her thinking to accommodate this new knowledge: Some dogs are small, but some are big.

Assimilation occurs when a child takes in various experiences and fits them into a current mental model for thinking or acting. For example, imagine that the same child in a different situation sees a big animal that barks. Because she now knows now that some dogs are big and some are small, she is able to assimilate this new information: The barking animal is a dog.

Piaget's theory identifies four stages of cognitive development: sensorimotor, preoperational, concrete operational, and formal operational. The sensorimotor stage and the preoperational stage are relevant to *The Creative Curriculum*®. Older children reach the concrete and formal operational stages.

The **sensorimotor stage** begins at birth and lasts until about age 2. In this stage, children learn by reacting to what they experience through their senses and physical activity, especially through manipulation of objects. For example, they put books in their mouths, kick play gyms with their feet, and pull at the strings of wheeled toys to discover what they can do with these objects. Through many interactions and opportunities to explore objects, they learn that a book has a cover and pages, that kicking a mobile will cause it to spin, and that pulling the string on a toy will bring it to them. Piaget thought that their motor development underlies their cognitive development.

When babies learn that the mother seen from the back and the mother seen from the front are the same mother and that a ball still exists when it rolls out of sight, they understand *object permanence.* This means that they understand that objects maintain their identities when they change location and usually continue to exist when they are out of sight.

At about age 2, children enter a stage that Piaget calls the **preoperational period.** During this stage, which lasts throughout the preschool years, children begin to notice the properties of the objects they explore. However, their observations are limited to only one attribute of an object at a time. They focus on how things look and do not use adult logic. For example, children at this stage may think that the tallest person in the room must also be the oldest. They are unable to understand that height and age do not always correspond directly.

Children who are at the preoperational stage also tend to see the world from their own point of view. Piaget calls this characteristic *egocentrism.* The following conversation is an example of egocentrism:

> "I'm going to read this book about trucks," the teacher explains. "I have a truck," says one child. Another comments, "My daddy drives a truck." "My daddy is tall," observes a third child. "I'm tall," responds a fourth.

Each child responds to what was said with information about himself, rather than staying with the other's idea.

Piaget believed that pretend play is essential to cognitive development during this stage. By taking on pretend roles and using objects in unconventional ways (for example, using a block as a telephone) children are thinking symbolically. Symbolic play experiences lay the foundation for more abstract symbolic thinking later, such as using letters, numbers and numerals, and words.

Recent research has also shown that child development is more fluid and more tied to specific content knowledge than Piaget's stages suggest. For instance, a child who thinks that the tallest person must be the oldest might often draw valid conclusions about other situations. She might conclude that not all men are daddies, because she has had many experiences with men who are daddies and men who are not. Nevertheless, the sequential development of logic that Piaget identified still holds. He also helped us understand the role of the child's actions in development. Piaget's descriptions of how children construct understanding inform the teaching techniques, selection of materials, and suggested experiences of *The Creative Curriculum®*.

Lev Vygotsky

The social aspect of children's cognitive development was a primary interest of Lev Vygotsky.[10] While Piaget paid more attention to the relationship between physical and cognitive development, Vygotsky recognized that social interaction is crucial to children's cognitive learning. According to Vygotsky, children grow cognitively not only by acting on objects but also by interacting with adults and more knowledgeable peers. Teachers' verbal directions, physical assistance, and probing questioning help children improve skills and acquire knowledge. Peers who have advanced skills can also help other children grow and learn by modeling strategies or providing other assistance.

Vygotsky uses the term *zone of proximal development* (ZPD) to describe the range of a child's learning about a particular experience. The lower limit of the zone is what a child can do independently. The upper limit of the zone is what a child can learn by watching and talking to peers and teachers. With the support of others, the child organizes new information to fit what he already knows. As a result, he can function at a higher level than he could by working on his own. This process of helping a child build knowledge and understanding is called *scaffolding*, just as a scaffold holds you up so you can reach a higher place when you are building a house.

To be able to scaffold children's learning, Vygotsky, like Piaget, taught that teachers need to be expert observers of children. By interacting with children, asking questions, and thinking carefully about children's development, teachers can determine each child's developmental level and consider ways to extend children's learning.

The Creative Curriculum® is grounded in Vygotsky's theory that social interaction is key to children's learning. Your primary role is to establish and maintain trusting relationships with children by being responsive to their individual needs. Learning takes place through positive relationships between and among children and adults. Planning and teaching is based on observing and documenting what children do and say. In Vygotsky's terms, you need to determine each child's ZPD. Then you can provide individualized experiences for children that are challenging enough to help them move to a higher level of learning but not so challenging as to frustrate them.

Brain Research

Brain research has improved our understanding of how and when children learn best. Experimental studies of animals and recent innovations in medical technology have led to many new insights. Here are some of the elements of brain research that inform *The Creative Curriculum*®.

What We Know From Brain Research	Implications for Teachers
Learning is not a matter of nature versus nurture; it is both. We used to think that heredity (a person's inborn characteristics) is more important than environment (what he or she is exposed to) in determining how well a person learns. In fact, both play a major role.	The ability to learn is not as fixed as we once thought. All children benefit from rich experiences and interactions in early childhood. Teachers can have a profound influence on all children's learning and development.
The human brain is affected by experiences. Children's learning changes the physical structure of their brains.	Every appropriate sensorimotor experience that teachers provide helps children build brain connections.
Learning needs to be reinforced again and again. For a brain connection to become permanent, it must be used repeatedly. Connections that are not used eventually disappear.	Children need many different opportunities to practice new skills. Rather than constantly rotating materials and interrupting children's repetitive play (such as dropping a block off a table and picking it up again and again), teachers give children time to practice new skills.
In order to learn, children need to feel safe and confident. Stress, on the other hand, can trigger chemical changes that begin in the brain and affect many processes in the body. The changes probably affect attention, memory, planning, and behavioral control.	Secure relationships with family members, teachers, and other significant people in a child's life are essential to learning. *The Creative Curriculum*® teachers make it their first priority to develop trusting, nurturing relationships with the children in their care.
Nutrition, health, and physical activity affect learning. Movement stimulates connections in the brain. A well-balanced diet, sufficient sleep, and plenty of exercise support healthy brain growth.	Daily exercise and time outdoors are essential for health and well-being, even for young infants. Many programs also provide health screening, as well as meals and snacks.

Theory and Research

What We Know From Brain Research	Implications for Teachers
Evidence shows that visual impairments, auditory deficits, and perceptual-motor delays have serious negative effects on children's developing nervous systems. There might also be sensitive periods when the brain is more receptive to certain types of learning (including emotional control, social attachment, and language), but questions about the brain areas involved in such learning are still being explored. It appears that the brain remains open to experiences, so interventions are important.[11]	Teachers focus on the skills that provide a foundation for all future learning and offer corrective efforts when children have disabilities. The development of self-regulation, skills for forming relationships with others, strategies for solving problems, language, and music should be important aspects of the curriculum.
During the early years, the brain is more receptive to phonology, learning the individual sounds that make up languages.	Teachers support children's phonological development and language acquisition by talking, singing, reading, and playing with the sounds of words. Dual-language learners are supported in learning their home languages as well as the primary language spoken in the program.

Brain research has found physical evidence to support what Maslow, Erikson, and other theorists have taught us. It shows that the wiring in children's brain development is positively affected when they are healthy and well fed; feel safe from threats; and have nurturing, stable relationships. Because of this research, *The Creative Curriculum*® emphasizes the primary role that teachers play.

Major Ideas	*The Creative Curriculum*®
Jean Piaget Children's logical thinking develops in stages. They need many opportunities to explore the world around them in order to refine their understandings about how things work. Infants learn by reacting to what they experience through their senses and physical activity. Toddlers and twos are egocentric (see things from their point of view) and overgeneralize their limited experiences.	• Provide safe opportunities for infants to explore their environment through play. • Create a system for collecting and sanitizing mouthed toys and materials, because infants use all of their senses to explore. • Provide opportunities for toddlers and twos to make choices. • Schedule uninterrupted periods of time for children to play and explore their environment. • Ask open-ended questions to encourage children's thinking.
Lev Vygotsky Interactions with teachers and peers are an important part of children's cognitive development. Teachers scaffold children's learning by offering assistance and giving supporting information. Teachers must observe children closely to understand how to support their learning.	• Observe children carefully. • Organize a system for recording observation notes and otherwise documenting children's development and learning. • Use information from your observations to plan routines and experiences that encourage children's development and learning. • Encourage social interaction between children with varying skill levels so that they can learn from one another. • Offer assistance to children as needed.
Learning and the Brain Knowledge of young children's cognitive development has grown with the newer understanding of how the brain develops. Brain development is affected by learning and experiences, which need to be repeated. Emotions, physical health, nutrition, and movement affect learning. There are sensitive periods when the brain is at its peak for certain kinds of learning, but the brain remains open to experiences. Early and sustained stress affects brain development negatively.[12]	• Provide many and varied experiences for children. • Allow children time to practice new skills. • Develop positive relationships with each child. • Create a safe environment where children can explore confidently and learn. • Provide many rich language experiences throughout the day, by describing what is happening, asking questions, singing, and reading. • Offer continuity of care and primary caregiving.

Knowing Infants, Toddlers, and Twos

What Infants, Toddlers, and Twos Are Like	**18**
Social–Emotional Development	18
Physical Development	21
Language Development	24
Cognitive Development	27
Individual Differences	**30**
Temperament	30
Life Circumstances	33
Dual-Language Learners	34
Disabilities	35

Knowing Infants, Toddlers, and Twos

The first 3 years of life are a time of tremendous development and learning. Think about a newborn baby. Every experience is new to her. Her reactions are limited to such things as turning her head toward what she likes (such as her mother's breast for feeding) or turning her head away from what she does not like (such as loud noises). She can relax her body and become quiet, or tense her body and cry. She depends completely on adults to take care of her and respond to her needs, to clean and feed her, move her, offer her the appropriate level of activity, and soothe her when she is upset.

Two and a half years later, the same child who once had only a few ways to communicate her needs has become a skilled communicator, pointing and using other gestures, and speaking in sentences. As she developed relationships with the important adults in her life, she began learning to relate to other people. In addition to observing actively, she can now manipulate, group, and sort objects. Her motor skills have progressed from the basic reflexive movements of a newborn to the complex skills of an energetic, running, climbing 2-year-old.

This chapter explains the first component of *The Creative Curriculum® for Infants, Toddlers & Twos*. Curriculum begins with knowing children.

There are two sections in this chapter:

What Infants, Toddlers, and Twos Are Like presents an overview of the developmental characteristics of children from birth to 36 months. Four areas of child development are discussed: social–emotional, physical, cognitive, and language. The influence of culture upon various aspects of child development is also examined briefly.

Individual Differences discusses the ways in which temperament, life circumstances, dual-language learning, and disabilities might affect the development of individual children.

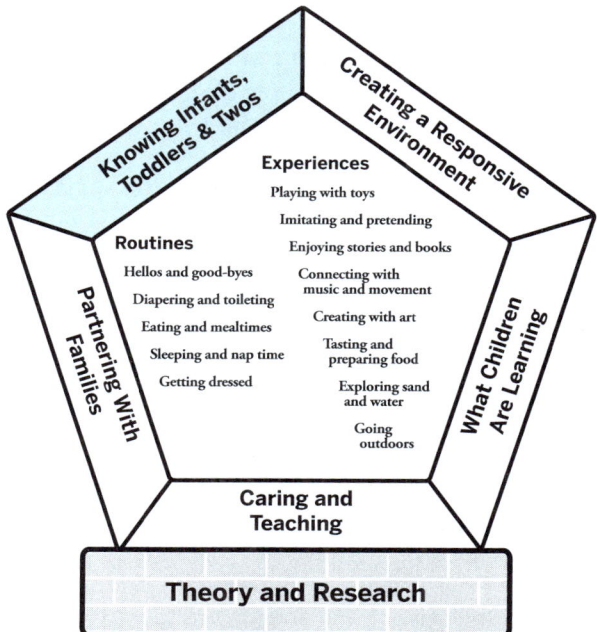

What Infants, Toddlers, and Twos Are Like

Child development information may be divided into four areas: social–emotional, physical, cognitive, and language. While it is helpful to consider these areas for planning and discussion, development does not really divide into neat categories. Rather, the four categories are closely related and often overlap. Development in one area affects and is influenced by development in all other areas. This is why teachers have to pay attention to all four areas.

> **Leo** (18 months) is developing expressive language. He approaches his teacher, Barbara, and says, "Up, p'ease." She promotes Leo's language development when she expands on his communication by saying, "You would like me to pick you up, please." She supports his social–emotional development when she returns Leo's smile and lifts him into her arms. Leo practices physical skills when he stands and raises his arms toward her. When she acts on this request, Barbara reinforces Leo's understanding of cause and effect, an important element of cognitive development.

The following sections provide an overview of the four areas of child development for children from birth to 36 months.

Social–Emotional Development

Young children's social–emotional development involves the way they feel about themselves, their understanding of feelings, their ability to regulate emotions and express them appropriately, and their capacity for building relationships with others. It flourishes when they have close, supportive, and trusting relationships with adults. When adults are responsive, when they share the pleasure of children's accomplishments and discoveries, and when they create an environment in which children can participate actively in daily routines and experiences, they show children that they are important, interesting, and competent. Through positive interactions, children learn about themselves and how to relate to others.

There are three objectives for social–emotional development and learning:

Objective 1. Regulates own emotions and behaviors
a. Manages feelings
b. Follows limits and expectations
c. Takes care of own needs appropriately

Objective 2. Establishes and sustains positive relationships
a. Forms relationships with adults
b. Responds to emotional cues
c. Interacts with peers
d. Makes friends

Objective 3. Participates cooperatively and constructively in group situations
a. Balances needs and rights of self and others
b. Solves social problems

Young infants have little ability to regulate their emotions. Initially, they express themselves by such things as turning slightly toward or away from what they like or dislike and by crying and smiling. With attentive, responsive care, infants quickly learn which behaviors lead to having their needs met, to being fed, being changed when soiled or wet, being comforted to sleep, and being held and loved.

Sometimes adults worry that they will spoil infants if they always respond to their needs. However, infants whose needs are met consistently and lovingly are more easily comforted, are better able to pay attention to what is going on around them, and are more open to exploring their environment and to new experiences. They also learn more quickly to calm themselves and regulate their emotions in other ways. Adults who do not respond to an infant's cries until the infant becomes extremely distressed encourage the baby to rise to a frantic level of crying more quickly in the future. This kind of delayed response makes it harder for parents and teachers to settle the baby and harder for the baby to learn to regulate his emotions.

At around 2 months, something wonderful happens. Babies smile for the first time. By 3 or 4 months, babies begin to laugh in response to very active stimuli.

> **Julio** (4 months) coos with laughter when Linda covers his toes with kisses and says, "Where are the baby's toes? ¿Dónde están los dedos del pie del bebé? Oh, there are the little toes. I'm going to gobble up those toes!"

At about 5–6 months, young infants begin to develop an understanding that they are separate individuals. As they explore, they pull at their parents' hair, study their teachers' faces, and reach for the jewelry or glasses worn by familiar adults.

Young infants are fascinated by other people and soon learn to use facial expressions, other movements, and vocalizations to initiate, return, and end interactions with others. With teachers who respond to their emotional and social cues (crying, laughing, smiling), infants begin to learn that they can affect others through their actions. This understanding helps them to see themselves as competent individuals who can influence the world around them.

By about 8 months of age, when most infants have established secure attachments with the important adults in their lives, they become upset when their preferred adult leaves (separation anxiety) and anxious when a new adult is present (stranger anxiety). They show their secure attachment to their parents and teachers with more intensified clinging. Their anxiety is usually resolved as infants become more mobile, spend more time away from the people to whom they first became securely attached, and develop close relationships with other important adults in their lives, such as their teachers.

Mobile infants are active, enthusiastic explorers who are in love with the world. They are often so busy crawling, cruising, walking, and practicing their other new skills that, to get their attention, their families sometimes have to stand in front of them and wave.

Mobile infants enjoy watching other children and begin to imitate each other. They also engage in *social referencing*, looking at others' faces, recognizing emotional expressions, and using this information to react to new situations and people.

> **Willard** (11 months) discovers a tray of water placed on a low table. He looks at Grace as if to ask, "May I play with this?" Grace smiles and nods encouragingly. Willard turns back to the tray and splashes it enthusiastically with his hand.

Mobile infants can also crawl or walk to their trusted teachers when they feel sad or frightened or just need some reassurance. Increased mobility gives them a new strategy for regulating their emotions (actively seeking protection and comfort from a teacher). Development of *emotional regulation* (in this case, increased awareness that a trusted teacher will help them if they become scared, sad, or unsure of themselves) also motivates them to master physical skills. This is another example of how all areas of development are related.

As their motor and cognitive abilities increase, mobile infants feel more capable. They want to control their actions and the effects those actions produce. When things do not go the way they would like—as when a favorite toy is out of reach, a pop-up toy does not pop up, or their hands are blocked from grabbing a fragile item—they react with frustration and sometimes anger. Their happiness is also powerful. When enjoying a toy, older mobile infants stop their play and smile with delight at a trusted adult to communicate their pleasure. A simple game of peek-a-boo may prompt lots of happy laughter.

Toddlers busily explore their independence as they learn about and respond increasingly appropriately to the feelings of others and as they gain better control over their emotions. The world is an exciting place for toddlers, but it sometimes overwhelms them. As a result, toddlers typically find themselves wanting the impossible: to be big and to stay little at the same time. The same toddler who screams, "No!" when his teacher says it is time to wash his hands may be crying five minutes later, wanting to be cuddled like a baby. Responsive and caring teachers understand that toddlers want to practice their new skills, make their own decisions, and do things themselves.

> **Matthew** (22 months) pushes Mercedes' hands out of the way and says, "No, me," when she tries to help him put on his coat. She listens to what Matthew is telling her. She asks, "Do you want to put your coat on by yourself?" and Matthew nods his head.

Twos' increased language skills provide them with a greater ability to regulate their emotions and explore their sense of self. They develop a vocabulary for talking about feelings and about themselves. While toddlers fondly use the words *me* and *mine,* twos are soon able to use words like *sad, mad, scary, love, silly,* and *yucky* to describe their thoughts and feelings. Being able to express their emotions to a responsive teacher gives them new control over their emotions and behavior. As twos become more self-aware and as they understand the expectations that adults have for their behavior, self-conscious emotions, such as shame, pride, and guilt, also develop. They also use this new understanding of emotions to empathize with others. Twos not only begin to use words to express their emotions, they can also recognize and respond appropriately to the emotions of others.

How Culture Might Affect Social–Emotional Development

Young children learn by observing the important people in their lives. Their families' home cultures greatly influence their understanding of which emotions to express and how and when to express them. Some cultures value the group's well-being over the individual's (collectivism). In these cultures, it is often more important not to express strong emotions in order to maintain the harmony of the group. Cultures that value the individual's well-being over the group's (individualism) tend to appreciate the expression of an individual's feelings, such as by smiling broadly, laughing loudly, crying mightily, or scowling deeply.

Culture may also determine whether children are encouraged to express pride about individual accomplishments or whether to feel shame or embarrassment at being recognized individually in front of a group. Families who value individualism often encourage children to express pride and happiness about personal accomplishments, whereas families who value collectivism might feel shame or embarrassment if someone calls attention to an individual's success in front of a group.

> **Barbara** knows that the majority of the families she serves have home cultures that value collectivism. She is therefore careful to share children's individual accomplishments with families when they are alone rather than with others.

Physical Development

Physical development refers to gradually gaining control over large and small muscles. Gross-motor (or large-muscle) skills allow a child to do such things as roll over, sit, crawl, walk, run, and throw a ball. Fine-motor (or small-muscle) skills, such as holding, pinching, and flexing fingers, eventually enable children to do such things as draw, write, eat with utensils, and cut with scissors. The development of new motor skills allows young children to make other new discoveries. As they explore, they begin to make sense of their environment.

> **Julio** (4 months), having gained control of his head, can better use his eyes and ears to locate the source of a sound.

> **Willard** (11 months) is able to use his fingers, hands, and wrists to touch, taste, and smell the slice of pear on the table.

> **Jonisha** (33 months) can turn the pages of her book one at a time. She identifies pictures of common objects and animals and recalls a familiar story.

Although they develop at different rates, infants learn to control their bodies in the same progression. Control develops from head to toe, and from the center of their bodies out through their arms and legs to their fingers and toes. You can see this general pattern as you watch a child learn to lift his head and then sit, crawl, walk, and run.

There are four objectives for physical development and learning:

Objective 4. Demonstrates traveling skills

Objective 5. Demonstrates balancing skills

Objective 6. Demonstrates gross-motor manipulative skills

Objective 7. Demonstrates fine-motor strength and coordination
a. Uses fingers and hands
b. Uses writing and drawing tools

Young infants move primarily by reflex when they are newborns. They move automatically in response to various stimuli. Some reflexes help ensure that infants will get what they need to survive. For example, when you touch the cheek of a newborn, she starts moving her mouth in search of a nipple. When you touch her mouth or when her mouth touches the nipple of a breast or bottle, she begins sucking. Young infants have other reflexes, too. For example, reciprocal kicking occurs when an infant kicks first one foot, then the other. This reflex suggests skills yet to be developed, such as crawling and walking. During the first eight months, however, infants change from having little control over their muscles to developing motor skills such as rolling over, reaching for and grasping objects, transferring items from hand to hand, sitting without help from an adult, and often beginning to crawl.

Mobile infants quickly become skilled at moving themselves from place to place. They pull themselves up to standing, using the support of furniture, toys, or a trusted adult. They begin to cruise from this upright position, holding onto the edges of furniture while walking. Next, they take their first steps and walk without support. When they are about a year old, they begin to stack blocks or other toys. Their *pincer grasp*—holding something with the thumb and index finger—becomes more coordinated, so they can pick up small pieces of cereal, turn knobs on toys, and open and close small boxes.

Toddlers have a wide range of gross- and fine-motor skills. They can walk and run, and they are developing new skills such as hopping and throwing balls.

> **Mercedes** notices that, now that Matthew (22 months) has begun to run, he usually runs from one activity to another, practicing this new skill.

Toddlers use their fingers and hands to put puzzle pieces in place; make marks with a crayon; roll, pound, and squeeze playdough; and paint.

Twos continue to refine their motor skills. They combine various gross-motor skills during play and move more easily from running to jumping to climbing. They begin to coordinate their arms and legs to try complicated tasks such as pedaling and steering a tricycle. As their fine-motor skills advance, their scribbling gets smaller and more controlled, and they enjoy stringing large beads to make necklaces.

> **Valisha** (33 months) refines her fine-motor skills as she begins to use scissors successfully to cut paper. LaToya notices this as she observes Valisha during art experiences.

Toddlers and twos need many opportunities and a safe environment to practice, refine, and master physical skills. You can promote motor development by encouraging children to try new skills and sometimes by helping them to slow down a little so they can gain more control.

How Culture Might Affect Physical Development

A family's cultural practices can influence the rate at which children develop motor skills. If a child's home culture believes strongly in independence, then a child may be encouraged to move in order to do things on her own at an earlier age. If a child's home culture values relationships with others more than personal independence, she may be discouraged from doing things independently at a young age.

> **Abby's** mother explains to Brooks that she spoon-feeds Abby at home and will probably continue to do so for several years. Abby's mother believes that this culturally supported practice is one way that she can show Abby (14 months) how much she loves her and how important it is for people to depend on and help each other.

Language Development

Language development is one of children's major accomplishments during the first 3 years of life. They progress from communicating needs through facial expressions, gestures, body movements, and crying to communicating through verbal or sign language. They can acquire a vocabulary of thousands of words and learn the rules for using them by being around and interacting with adults who communicate with them, encourage their efforts to communicate, and guide their exploration and learning.

Learning to talk takes practice. By sharing your pleasure in children's communication rather than correcting their mistakes, and by talking with them even before they understand what you are saying or can respond verbally, you help children build on their desire to communicate.

There are three objectives for language development and learning:

Objective 8. Listens to and understands increasingly complex language

a. Comprehends language
b. Follows directions

Objective 9. Uses language to express thoughts and needs

a. Uses an expanding expressive vocabulary
b. Speaks clearly
c. Uses conventional grammar
d. Tells about another time or place

Objective 10. Uses appropriate conversational and other communication skills

a. Engages in conversations
b. Uses social rules of language

There are two additional objectives for English language acquisition:

Objective 37. Demonstrates progress in listening to and understanding English

Objective 38. Demonstrates progress in speaking English

Young infants are born with a unique ability to relate to other human beings. They come into the world ready to communicate. A newborn turns her head to the sound of her mother's voice. When their eyes meet, the baby's face brightens and quiets. Infants cry to communicate their needs, but crying is not their only means of communication. During the first few months, they begin making other sounds as well. They gurgle, coo, and squeal, using sounds to initiate, continue, and end interactions with others. By about 6–9 months, infants begin to babble language sounds, practicing rising and falling intonation, and experimenting with volume. By age 1, they focus on their own culture's language rather than the full range of sounds used in the world's languages.[13] In addition to making sounds, infants also listen and respond.

As they get older, infants respond by smiling, kicking, and turning their heads to look at someone who is talking. They also cry, turn away, or withdraw when they are unhappy with their environments.

Mobile infants are able to understand much more than they can say. Before they are able to talk, they look at objects you name and make gestures, such as waving good-bye when someone leaves or pointing at a book that is just out of reach. They can respond to requests and questions by using gestures, sounds, and sometimes words.

> **Brooks** asks Abby (14 months) if she would rather have apples or pears with her lunch. Abby points to the apples and says, "Appa."

At about age 1, some mobile infants say a few recognizable words, usually the names of people and things that are important to them. In English-speaking families, early words often include *mama*, *dada*, *ba* (for bottle), *bow-wow*, or *ball*. Children soon start to mix words and babble, speaking with great expression.

Mobile infants enjoy looking at pictures in books, particularly illustrations of familiar things: people's faces, babies, toys, trucks, and animals. You can help them build strong vocabularies by sharing books with them and naming the objects in pictures. Mobile infants like turning the pages of their favorite books and pointing to familiar pictures when you offer prompts.

Toddlers continue to understand much more than they can say, and they are able to listen to and enjoy more complex stories.

> **Matthew** (22 months) giggles in response to a book that Mercedes reads about a dog who loves to dance.

Many toddlers have at least 50 words in their expressive vocabularies by the time they are 18 months old.[14] Estimates of children's expressive vocabularies (the words they say) vary widely at age 2, but researchers agree that young children's receptive vocabularies (the words they understand when they hear them) are much larger. Mobile infants learn that one of the functions of language is to help them get what they want or need. They begin putting two words together to express other thoughts as well, such as "Daddy go" or "Me do."

Twos continue to increase their language skills, both their ability to listen (receptive language) and their ability to speak (expressive language). Between the ages of 2 and 3 years, their vocabularies continue to increase dramatically, and their sentences become more complex. They engage in conversations, offering ideas and asking questions.

As their language skills develop, so does their interest in and ability to talk about books.

> **Gena** (30 months) says, "Night Moon," as she brings the book Goodnight Moon to Ivan every afternoon before she naps. **Jonisha** and **Valisha** (33 months) enjoy choosing books from the shelf, turning the pages, and telling the story to each other from memory.

How Culture Might Affect Language Development

As in all other aspects of development, young children's use of speech varies. Some say their first words at 8 months, while others hardly speak at all until they are almost 2 years old. Many factors influence how and when language develops. Some are individual differences present from birth. Others depend on a child's experiences with language and whether a child is learning two languages at once. Dual-language learning is discussed in the next section.

A child's home culture can influence when a child speaks and the way in which he uses verbal language, facial expressions, gestures, and silence to communicate. Some families rely heavily on verbal language and direct speech. Others rely more on the facial expressions of the speaker and on indirect communication strategies. Children reared by families who value direct communication and who use many words to explain a situation or to express thoughts and feelings will probably use speech in the same way.

A child whose family culture values indirect communication is generally physically closer to his parents (being carried, sitting on a lap, or touching a family member). That physical closeness allows the adult to read the child's body signals—a change in position, a tensing of the muscles, a subtle change in expression—and respond to them. This encourages the child to continue to communicate nonverbally rather than relying on words. Understanding these different styles will help you to recognize each child's communication attempts and better support the language development of the children in your care.

Cognitive Development

Cognitive development involves the way children think, develop understandings about the world, and use what they learn to reason and solve problems. Infants, toddlers, and twos interact with others and use all of their senses and motor skills actively to construct their own understandings about the people and objects in their environment. Children learn when they roll over, crawl around and over everything in their paths, run, jump, knock things over, and pick things up. They learn as they grasp a rattle, pound playdough, and smell the grilled cheese sandwiches you make for lunch. They learn as they play and as they live their everyday lives with you and their families. As they eat, get dressed, have their diapers changed, sit on a toilet, or move a chair across the room, they collect information about how things work.

There are four objectives for cognitive development and learning:

Objective 11. Demonstrates positive approaches to learning
a. Attends and engages
b. Persists
c. Solves problems
d. Shows curiosity and motivation
e. Shows flexibility and inventiveness in thinking

Objective 12. Remembers and connects experiences
a. Recognizes and recalls
b. Makes connections

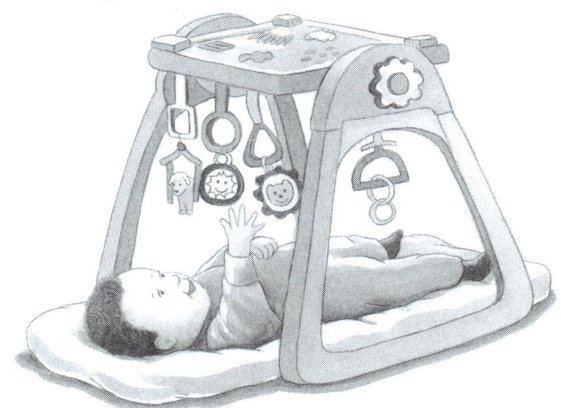

Objective 13. Uses classification skills

Objective 14. Uses symbols and images to represent something not present
a. Thinks symbolically
b. Engages in sociodramatic play

Young infants are experiencing everything for the first time and are trying to make sense of their world. Their ability to focus on and explore objects increases as their vision and grasp develops.

As infants are able to sit up, reach for toys, and explore things with their hands and mouths, they experiment with such properties as soft and hard, smooth and rough, heavy and light, and big and little.

When they consistently experience predictable routines, young infants learn to anticipate events. For example, an infant who is crying because he is wet might stop crying when he sees you pick up a diaper. He has learned that, when you pick up a diaper, his discomfort will end soon. Infants also learn that they can control their environments when they intentionally try to repeat something interesting that they originally did unintentionally. A child who pushes a car accidentally and likes the way it rolls may pound on the car, touch it, and knock it over before he tries pushing it again. He is beginning to understand the connection between his pushing and the car's rolling.

> **Jasmine** (8 months) opens and closes a cupboard door repeatedly, making it bang. She learns that her repeated behavior affects objects in consistent ways. This understanding helps her to make sense of her world.

Mobile infants begin to show their increasing ability to act intentionally, use tools, and understand cause and effect. They learn that particular actions have particular results. They continue to build understandings about cause and effect and use new problem-solving skills.

> **Willard** (11 months) wants the pull toy that is on the other side of the table. He gets it by pulling the string. He has learned that pulling the string makes the toy attached to the string move.

Children this age often imitate the actions of others.

> **Abby** (14 months) bangs a drum as she watches Leo doing so.

As children learn more and more about the world and the objects in it, they begin to categorize new information. Once mobile infants begin talking, they frequently ask, "Dat?" as they try to collect more information about the new things they encounter.

Toddlers' developing language and memory skills affect other aspects of their thinking. For example, they can separate from their families more easily because they have begun to understand that people leave and come back. As their ability to remember events and people increases, they engage in lots of pretend play, exploring daily and special events and social roles.

Children at this age tend to be egocentric. This means that they believe that they can control the world and that everyone thinks and feels as they do. For example, a toddler may believe he can make the traffic on a busy street come to a standstill, simply by yelling, "Stop!" Toddlers also believe that all moving things are alive.

> **Leo** (18 months) is afraid of the sounds of a flushing toilet and a running vacuum cleaner, believing that these objects are alive because they make such loud sounds and have moving parts.

Twos are better able to collect new information and link it to what they already know. As they push a play vacuum cleaner around the room, they discover that they can control the toy, just as you control the real vacuum. With consistent, predictable routines, they begin to understand basic concepts about time and to recognize that there is an order to daily events.

> **Valisha** (33 months) begins looking for her parents after story time, knowing that they usually arrive after that time of the day.

As their attention span increases, twos are able to persist with more complex problem solving and may investigate the cause when something unexpected happens.

> **Gena** (30 months) is building a block tower. She places a large block on top of a stack of small blocks, and the tower falls to the ground. She looks at it with a frown and says, "Blocks fell down." After a few minutes of stacking and unstacking the blocks, Gena begins to rebuild the tower with the large block on the bottom.

How Culture Might Affect Cognitive Development

A child's home culture can influence the way he learns and processes new information. Cultures encourage children to explore their environments in different ways. In some cultures, experimenting with toys, manipulating objects, and solving problems by using materials are highly valued as the way children learn best. Other cultures value observation more than handling materials. In some communities, children learn by observing their environments, watching others interact, and focusing on people rather than materials.

> **Mercedes** has a toddler in her class whose family values observation more than active manipulation of objects. She frequently sees him standing or sitting in one place, focusing intently on an interaction between adults or other children. She knows that, if she approaches and encourages him to interact with the others or tries to distract him with a toy or game, she would interrupt his way of learning. By talking with this child's family, Mercedes has come to understand how much he learns when he watches intently.

Individual Differences

Your understanding of individual differences helps you build a trusting relationship with each child and makes each child feel comfortable in your care. Children have different temperaments, prior experiences, and life circumstances. Some may be learning English at the same time as they are learning their home language (dual-language learners). Some children have formally identified special needs.

Think about the children in your care. Perhaps you have an infant who loves to explore her environment and who opens every drawer, cabinet, and box she gets her hands on. She never seems to stop moving, even during nap time. Perhaps you have a toddler who hides behind his mother's legs and needs constant encouragement and support to interact with others and play with new toys.

Understanding children means appreciating their unique ways of interacting with the world and with people. It means taking time to learn about children's strengths, interests, challenges they like, challenges that frustrate them, and ways they are comforted. With this knowledge, you can respond in ways that address each child's needs. The planning forms discussed in the next chapter give you a way to use what you learn about each child and your group of children.

Temperament

Children are born with behavioral styles called *temperaments*. For example, some children approach new situations cautiously, without a fuss, and adapt slowly. Others have an immediate positive response to new situations, are generally cheerful, and have regular patterns of behavior. Still others withdraw or cry in new situations. When you are aware of a child's temperament, you can sometimes predict how that child will behave in certain types of situations. Thinking about temperament may help you to understand and interpret children's behaviors.

Research suggests that temperamental differences can be identified even in newborns. There are significant differences in the way babies respond to different stimuli, such as to loud noises or gentle rocking. Stella Chess and Alexander Thomas examined how the temperament of newborns influenced the further development of some personality traits.[15]

1. **Activity level**—How active is the child? Does he kick vigorously or is he often still? Does he squirm while having his diaper changed? Does he prefer to explore the world by watching and listening or by crawling and climbing?

2. **Biological rhythms**—How predictable are the child's sleeping and eating habits? Does he wake up, get hungry, and get sleepy at the same times each day?

3. **Tendency to approach or withdraw**—Does the child respond positively to (approach) something new or does she pull away (withdraw) from it? When something new happens, does she fuss, do nothing, or seem to like it? For example, does she reach for a new toy or push it away? Does she swallow a new food or spit it out? Does she smile at a new person or cry and move away?

4. **Adaptability**—How does the child react to change? Does he have a hard time with changes in routines or with new people? How long does it take him to get used to new foods, new people, and other new circumstances?

5. **Sensory threshold**—At what point does a child become bothered by noise or light, changes in temperature, different tastes, or the feel of clothing?

6. **Intensity or energy level of reactions**—How does the child respond emotionally? Does she react loudly and dramatically to even the most minor disappointment, or does she become quiet when she is upset?

7. **Mood**—Does the child have a positive or negative outlook? Is she generally in a light-hearted mood, or does she take things very seriously?

8. **Distractibility**—Is the child readily distracted from a task by what is going on around her? When being fed her bottle, does she turn her head to look in the direction of every new sound she hears or movement she sees?

9. **Persistence**—How long does the child stay with a task when it is challenging? How does he react to interruptions or requests to clean up when he is playing?

Children with different personality traits need to be treated differently.

> **Julio** (4 months) has very predictable eating and sleeping patterns. Linda knows to have his bottle ready at 2:00 when he wakes up from his nap.

> **Gena** (30 months) tends to be cautious in group situations. Knowing this, Ivan makes sure to invite her to play with him and another child every day.

While temperament may be inborn, providing appropriate support for children can help them function comfortably. An active child can calm down, and a child who tends to withdraw can learn strategies for feeling more comfortable in group situations.

Life Circumstances

In addition to other individual differences, varying life circumstances contribute to the uniqueness of each child. Consider how each of these factors affects the children you care for and teach.

Life Circumstances That May Affect Children's Development and Learning

- family composition, including the number and gender of parents, guardians, and other family members present in the home
- child's birth order, including the number and spacing of siblings
- presence of the chronic health problem or disability of a family member
- exposure to violence, abuse, addiction, or neglect
- home languages
- family cultural practices
- type of community in which the child lives
- kinds of work family members do
- age at which parents gave birth to or adopted their first child
- family economic status
- living situation, including history of moving
- parent's/guardian's level of education
- parent's/guardian's job history, including work-related travel
- special circumstances such as marital separation and divorce, absence of a family member for reasons not directly related to marriage, birth or adoption of a new sibling, how many different people and places the child experiences each day

Try to be aware of each child's circumstances when he or she enters your program. Your program's enrollment forms may be helpful in learning more about individual families. Talking with family members and taking notes about what you learn is an important first step. Encourage families to communicate with you about anything new taking place in children's lives, and honor their styles of communication. This process will take time as you develop a trusting relationship with family members. Remember to honor the confidentiality of information that family members share with you. If a family shares information with you that you do not know how to handle, seek advice from your supervisor or an outside expert.

Dual-Language Learners

Children whose home language is not English are very likely to be in your care, if not now, then in the future. The number of children who speak a first language that is not English (English-language learners) or who are learning English at the same time they are learning another language (dual-language learners) has increased dramatically and continues to increase in the United States.

Young children in your program may be learning two or more languages simultaneously, English in your program and another language or languages at home. Children may arrive in your classroom without ever having heard English anywhere other than on television, which is not a very good teacher. You may have several children who share a common home language other than English, or you may have children whose first languages are rare in your community.

Just as all children have very different strengths and needs, children who are learning English while they are learning another language vary greatly. The extent of children's knowledge of their primary language can vary, just as it does for children who speak only English at home.

Some children have language-rich home environments and arrive with strong language skills in their primary language. Other children have a weaker foundation on which to build language skills. Immersing them in a language-rich environment while they are in your care can help them increase their skills.

A number of misconceptions about learning two languages can cause unnecessary anxiety for teachers and parents. The following chart dispels some of these common misunderstandings.[16]

Misunderstandings About Dual-Language Learning

Misunderstandings	Reality
Children who are exposed to more than one language are at a clear disadvantage.	Bilingual children are often very creative and good at problem solving. Compared with children who speak one language, those who are bilingual can communicate with more people, read more, and benefit more from travel. Such children will have an additional skill when they enter the workforce.
Learning two languages at the same time confuses a child.	Children do not get confused, even when they combine languages in one sentence. Mixing languages is a normal and expected part of learning and speaking two languages.
Learning two languages as a young child will slow down children's readiness to read.	Actually, the opposite is often true. Because they have been exposed to the sounds and letter combinations of two languages, they usually learn to decode words well.
When children are exposed to two languages, they never become as proficient in either language as children who have to master only one language.	As long as they consistently use both languages, children can become proficient in both languages.
Only the brightest children can learn two languages without encountering problems. Most children have difficulty because the process is so complex.	Nearly all children are capable of learning two languages during the early childhood years. While the process may be complex for adults, young children's brains are still developing the structures for language, so they are able to learn multiple languages.

Specific strategies for supporting dual-language learners are discussed in other chapters. Exposure to rich language experiences in two languages is a definite asset. All children can benefit from learning another language.

Disabilities

All children have needs. However, you may feel more comfortable meeting some needs than others. For example, you may have several ideas for helping a child who has difficulty saying good-bye to his parents in the morning or for helping another who has temper tantrums. At the same time, you may be hesitant about working with a child who has cerebral palsy or who is visually impaired. You may wonder, "How can I ever meet the needs of these children?" Considering how to meet the needs of all children in your program is challenging. However, with an understanding of their individual development and the support of other professionals, you can help all children develop and learn.

Children are identified for special services in many ways. A child may be identified as having a disability at birth; during a checkup at the pediatrician's office; by a specialist such as a physical therapist; or by someone providing care and education, such as you.

Under Part C of The Individuals with Disabilities Education Act (IDEA), state or community teams work with family members to create an Individualized Family Service Plan (IFSP). These teams may include speech and physical therapists, physicians, social workers, public health nurses, and educators. Federal law (Public Law 108-446, 2004) requires that IFSPs contain this information:

- current developmental information, including a detailed account of a child's abilities and emerging skills
- desired developmental outcomes for the child on which team members agree
- desired developmental outcomes for the family on which team members agree
- a listing of the resources and services necessary to meet the unique needs of the child and family and a description of the environment in which these services will be provided
- specific developmental objectives that allow team members to see what progress is being made
- for children 30–36 months, a transition plan to support the children as they move to preschool or other appropriate services

The emphasis in *The Creative Curriculum*® on building trusting relationships is extremely important for young children with disabilities and their families. Some children may have been isolated because their families were anxious about bringing their child into the world beyond their home. Some of the children with disabilities in your group may receive special services, such as occupational, physical, or speech and language therapy. Invite specialists in these fields to your program to share ideas about common goals, strategies, and expectations.

Your involvement with a local early intervention program may come about in a variety of ways. You may be the person who suspects a developmental delay and initiates the intervention process by suggesting to the family that they call the state's Part C Coordinator, who will help them contact local service providers. You may know about a family's IFSP because you were contacted as the family's primary entry point into the system and have been involved from the beginning. Perhaps you were overlooked when the IFSP was written, or you might be meeting the family for the first time. If so, talk with the child's family about requesting a time to discuss their child's IFSP goals and adding your name to the team. You are an important member of the early intervention team because you work with the child each day to achieve developmental goals.

Federal legislation requires each state to have a lead agency with central responsibility for early intervention and a central directory of services. More information about Part C and how it can support the children and families in your program is available from The Council for Exceptional Children (www.cec.sped.org). The central office of your local public schools is another good resource.

The Americans with Disabilities Act requires child care providers to make reasonable accommodations to care for children with disabilities. This includes children who have chronic medical conditions, such as asthma, seizures, and sickle cell disease. Work with the child's family and health care providers to develop a detailed Individualized Health Plan (IHP) for the child. The IHP details all the accommodations needed for feeding, explains routine medication and other health procedures, outlines measures to prevent medical crises, and includes information about recognizing and responding to medical emergencies. You will also need to have the necessary medication and supplies, participate in training in the necessary health procedures, and have an emergency backup plan.

When working with children who have disabilities, first think about their strengths. Also learn about each child's interests before considering the child's special needs. Remember that there are individual differences in the way a disability affects each child.

> **Gena's** parents were nervous about what to expect when she entered the program for the first time. Ivan put them at ease by asking Gena (30 months) about the stuffed lamb she was carrying before talking with them about Gena's impaired speech and dexterity. During that conversation, Ivan learned that, while Gena's cerebral palsy affects her motor development, her cognitive development is typical for a child her age.

All children need to feel included and successful. For this to happen, you must look beyond the specific diagnosis to see how the disability affects the particular child. Be careful not to make assumptions about the child because of the diagnosis, although it is important to learn about the usual effects of the child's specific disability. Consider how a specific disability may or may not affect the child's daily life in your program. Use this information to decide what adjustments you need to make, if any. For example, you may need another adult to help you during certain parts of the day, or you may need to move furniture so a child's special equipment will fit in every part of your room.

Conclusion

Knowing how infants, toddlers, and twos develop is the starting point for planning your program, selecting materials, and guiding children's development and learning. While all areas of development are interrelated, they are usually discussed in terms of four areas: social–emotional, physical, language, and cognitive. In addition to knowing how children typically develop in these areas, teachers must also learn about the unique characteristics of each child. They must consider each child's temperament, life circumstances, the implications of a child's learning two or more languages, and the impact of a disability. The more you know about each child, the more you can appreciate a child's special qualities and use that knowledge to build a positive relationship. Knowledge of child development and individual children will also help you create a responsive environment that meets the needs of infants, toddlers, and twos. Setting up effective learning environments is addressed in the next chapter.

Creating a Responsive Environment

Setting Up the Physical Environment	**40**
Creating Places for Routines and Experiences	41
Designing Spaces for Each Age-Group	43
Selecting Materials	50
Displaying Materials	52
Special Considerations in Setting Up the Physical Environment	53
Sending Positive Messages	58
Creating a Structure for Each Day	**61**
Planning a Daily Schedule	61
Individualizing the Schedule for Infants	62
Schedules for Toddlers and Twos	66
Planning for Transitions	69
Responsive Planning	70

Creating a Responsive Environment

Your knowledge of the social–emotional, physical, cognitive, and language development of infants, toddlers, and twos and the many ways in which each child is unique enables you to create an environment that addresses the needs and growing abilities and interests of young children. Creating a responsive environment is the second component of *The Creative Curriculum® for Infants, Toddlers & Twos*.

This chapter discusses the environment in which you care for children and welcome families. It includes two sections:

Setting Up the Physical Environment explains how to arrange a welcoming place for children and families, and a pleasant, efficient place in which to work. It describes ways to create places for routines and experiences, discusses the design of spaces for each age-group, and offers guidelines for selecting and displaying materials. Special environmental considerations and ways the environment conveys positive messages to children and families are also discussed.

Creating a Structure for Each Day explains daily and weekly planning, individualizing the schedule for infants, and creating a schedule for toddlers and twos. Transitions and responsive planning are also included.

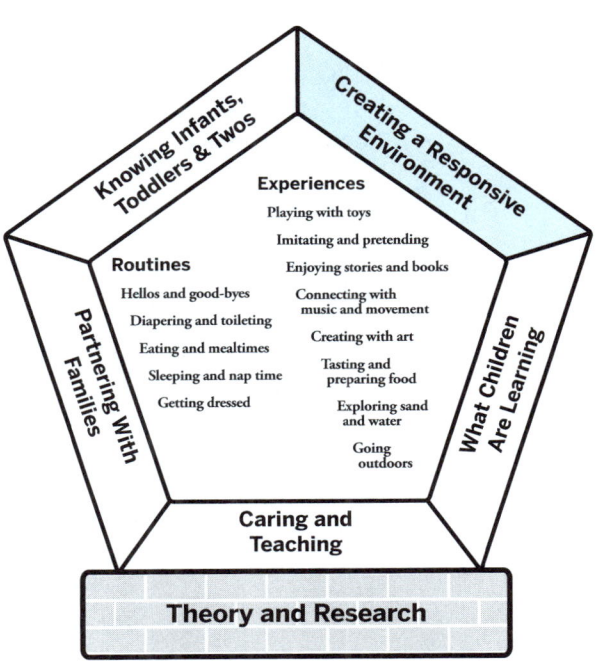

Setting Up the Physical Environment

A well-planned room for infants, toddlers, or twos is a welcoming place for children and families, and a pleasant, efficient place in which to work. Children spend many hours in your program. They are most comfortable when they are in a place that includes sights and sounds that are like those of their own homes. A child care environment that is similar to their homes encourages the feelings of safety and security that young children experience with their families.

A warm and friendly environment is also reassuring to families. Areas designed with family members in mind send the message that they are always welcome. Families can share ideas for making your environment more homelike, and they might be willing to contribute items and skills.

The next box outlines general space-planning guidelines that are discussed further in other sections of this chapter.

Space-Planning Guidelines

- Arrange the room so that all children can be seen at all times.
- Identify space for each of the routines and experiences.
- Organize the room efficiently.
- Clearly define spaces that need protection, such as spaces where infants will be playing on the floor.
- Establish traffic patterns and define pathways with low dividers if necessary.
- Locate active, noisier play areas and materials away from relatively quiet areas.
- Choose floor surfaces, such as carpeting or vinyl, according to the way the area will be used.
- Include comfortable places for adults.
- Create a variety of levels for infants, toddlers, and twos to explore.
- Provide light from a variety of sources.

Creating Places for Routines and Experiences

Areas that are conveniently located, organized, and well-equipped make routines easier to manage and allow you to focus on your interactions with children. Areas for experiences also need to be arranged according to the strengths and needs of the children.

Greeting Area

Locate the greeting area just inside the room. It serves as an entryway and a transition area between the outdoors or hallway and the room. Separate this area from the rest of the space to make it feel cozy and welcoming. It should be large enough to accommodate two or more parents with their children. Here are some items that will make your greeting area welcoming and functional:

- a bulletin- or message board for family notices
- cubbies or a coat rack and individual storage tubs
- photos of the children at play and with their families
- children's artwork
- a bench or counter at adult-height to make it easier to dress and undress children
- comfortable seating for two or more adults

Diapering and Toileting Areas

One of the challenges of organizing a diapering area is setting it up so you can see what the other children in the group are doing while you are changing a child's diaper. Ideally, the space should be designed so that you face the room—rather than a wall—while diapering. If this is not possible, place a mirror on the wall so that you can see behind you. Infant and toddler teachers spend a lot of time in the diapering area, so choose a convenient location. Handwashing is an integral part of diapering, so locate the diaper-changing table near a hand sink, and, to prevent the spread of disease, away from food-preparation areas. Storage is essential because you need to have many supplies nearby. In your diapering area, include

- storage for bleach solution, diapers, wipes, and extra clothing
- a safe changing table with a smooth, easily cleaned surface and a raised rim
- steps for older infants and toddlers to climb to the changing table
- a lined diaper can

Toddlers and twos often prefer to stand to be diapered. Check with your local licensing organization for ways to accommodate this preference while making sure that the diapering process is sanitary and safe.

Twos and their teachers spend a lot of time in the bathroom, so make it a pleasant place. Ideally, bathrooms are inside classrooms and have child-sized toilets, sinks, and paper towel holders so children can learn to function in the area independently. If you do not have child-size fixtures, the American Academy of Pediatrics and the American Public Health Association recommend that you use modified toilet seats and step aids for toilet learning. The use of potty chairs is discouraged because they are difficult to clean and sanitize. If you use potty chairs, follow the guidance on cleaning and sanitizing them.[17]

Sleeping Area

Some programs have separate sleeping areas for infants in cribs, while others incorporate cribs into the general space. Your state licensing requirements and the design of your facility will determine your options. Ideally, your sleeping area will be separate from noisy, active play areas so it can accommodate each child's individual sleeping schedule and preferences. If infants sleep within the classroom, you can group a few cribs together, creating the atmosphere of a bedroom rather than of an institution. By the time they are toddlers, children sleep on cots or mats that are set in the play areas of the room. Reserve some space for one or two children who sleep on a different schedule from the other children in the group. In your sleeping area, include

- lighting that can be dimmed
- storage space for sheets, blankets, and children's comfort items
- a glider or other comfortable chair for cuddling children and for watching them as they nap or play quietly
- a compact disc player for soft music

Nursing Area

The nursing area can be part of your sleeping area, or it can be located in another quiet area of the room. The nursing area should have comfortable seating, a footstool, and a small pillow to support the nursing mother's arm. A small folding screen or room divider provides some privacy.

Eating Area

A separate eating area is not necessary for young infants. Create quiet comfortable places where you can hold young infants while you feed them their bottles without being interrupted or distracted by other children. Mobile infants, toddlers, and twos need a space for eating, although the space can also used for play experiences such as dabbling in art or tasting and preparing food. Make sure that the eating area is separated from the diapering area.

A well-equipped eating and food preparation area includes

- a washable floor
- a counter and cupboards for storing food, dishes, and utensils
- a sink (preferably a double sink, which is convenient during mealtimes and for washing and sanitizing toys)
- a small refrigerator

- assigned space for each child's food in the cupboard and refrigerator, if families provide food, formula, or breast milk
- tables and chairs where mobile infants, toddlers, and twos can eat together in small groups (Once infants can sit comfortably and no longer need to be held to be fed, they can sit in sturdy chairs at low tables, rather than in high chairs.)
- a counter or cart that is large enough to hold serving dishes
- a comfortable place for teachers to sit if bottle-feeding children
- safety latches on lower cabinets, unless the entire storage area is inaccessible to children

Areas for Experiences

Chapters 11–18 discuss a variety of play experiences that infants, toddlers, and twos enjoy. These include playing with toys, imitating and pretending, enjoying stories and books, connecting with music and movement, creating with art, tasting and preparing food, exploring sand and water, and going outdoors. While all of these experiences require particular supplies and materials, not all require separate space. The next section provides information about how to design appropriate spaces for each age group.

Designing Spaces for Each Age-Group

One of the most important ways to put your knowledge of child development into practice is to design spaces that accommodate children's developmental needs, abilities, and interests. As infants, toddlers, and twos develop and learn, you will need to change the environment to keep children safe, provide new challenges, and inspire new interests.

Setting Up a Room for Young Infants

The infant room is a place where infants and adults can be comfortable and interact positively with each other. The youngest infants need soft, comfortable places throughout the room and a variety of views. Good, variable lighting is important. Take advantage of natural light whenever possible and consider using diffusers that minimize the glare from ceiling fixtures.

Arrange several protected areas where infants can watch the action from the floor. Provide soft toys for children to choose. As children develop, plan changes and additions to the environment. The next chart lists some characteristics of young infants and describes ways to arrange the environment to support their development and learning.

What Young Infants Can Do	Ways You Can Arrange the Environment	How This Supports Development
Notice and look at what is around them	Place pictures at children's eye level on the wall, ends of cribs, and shelves (including eye level when seated on an adult's lap and when held by a standing adult).	Encourages infants to focus and attend to objects
Distinguish familiar from unfamiliar sights and sounds	Provide familiar items, such as clothing, taped voices, and music.	Comforts infants with sights and sounds from home
Reach for, bat, and poke objects; grasp objects that can be held easily	Place toys within infants' reach.	Encourages infants to practice fine motor skills; encourages children to explore objects and notice how they react
Bring toys to their mouths to explore	Include a container for toys that need to be washed after play.	Supports exploration while keeping children healthy
Respond to being held and rocked	Have comfortable seating for when adults hold infants, such as soft chairs and gliders.	Builds trusting relationships
Develop the ability to roll, sit, and crawl	Provide soft surfaces, such as carpets, mats, and grass, so infants can move safely.	Promotes gross motor skills

Setting Up a Room for Mobile Infants

One of the most important things to remember in setting up an environment for mobile infants is that they move from place to place. They need protected spaces where they can crawl; low, carpeted risers that they can navigate; secure railings that they can pull on to stand and hold to cruise; and spaces where they can walk, fall safely, and walk again.

Many aspects of the environment for young infants are also appropriate for mobile infants. For example, soft areas and places to sit with adults continue to be important as children become more mobile. Even though mobile infants can move on their own, they still need adults to comfort and cuddle them.

Mobile infants are beginning to have preferences and like to choose what to play with and what to do. Organize the room to offer different play experiences, such as places to play with toys, roll balls, and look at books. You might also designate a few areas for experiences such as imitating and pretending.

The next chart lists some characteristics of mobile infants and suggests ways to arrange the environment to promote their development and learning.

What Mobile Infants Can Do	Ways You Can Arrange the Environment	How This Supports Development
Pull themselves to a standing position	Be sure furniture is sturdy, with rounded edges. Provide railings that children can use to pull themselves up.	Allows mobile infants to explore safely and to gain balance
Repeat a movement to learn it well	Provide space and time so children can play without being disturbed.	Encourages the development of attention and of motor skills
Push, pull, fill, and dump objects	Offer a variety of playthings and containers, including household objects.	Builds motor skills, eye-hand coordination, and a beginning understanding of cause and effect
Take comfort from familiar objects and reminders of home	Display pictures of family members and invite families to make audiotapes.	Strengthens secure attachments by helping children feel connected to their families throughout the day
Use familiar adults as a base for exploration	Use low dividers so children and adults can see each other while the children explore freely.	Helps children feel safe and secure

Chapter 2: **Creating a Responsive Environment**

There are many ways to set up a room for both young and mobile infants. Here is a sample layout to help you to think about your own infant room. Make sure you have enough open space. Infants are little, but they need space to move around and explore.

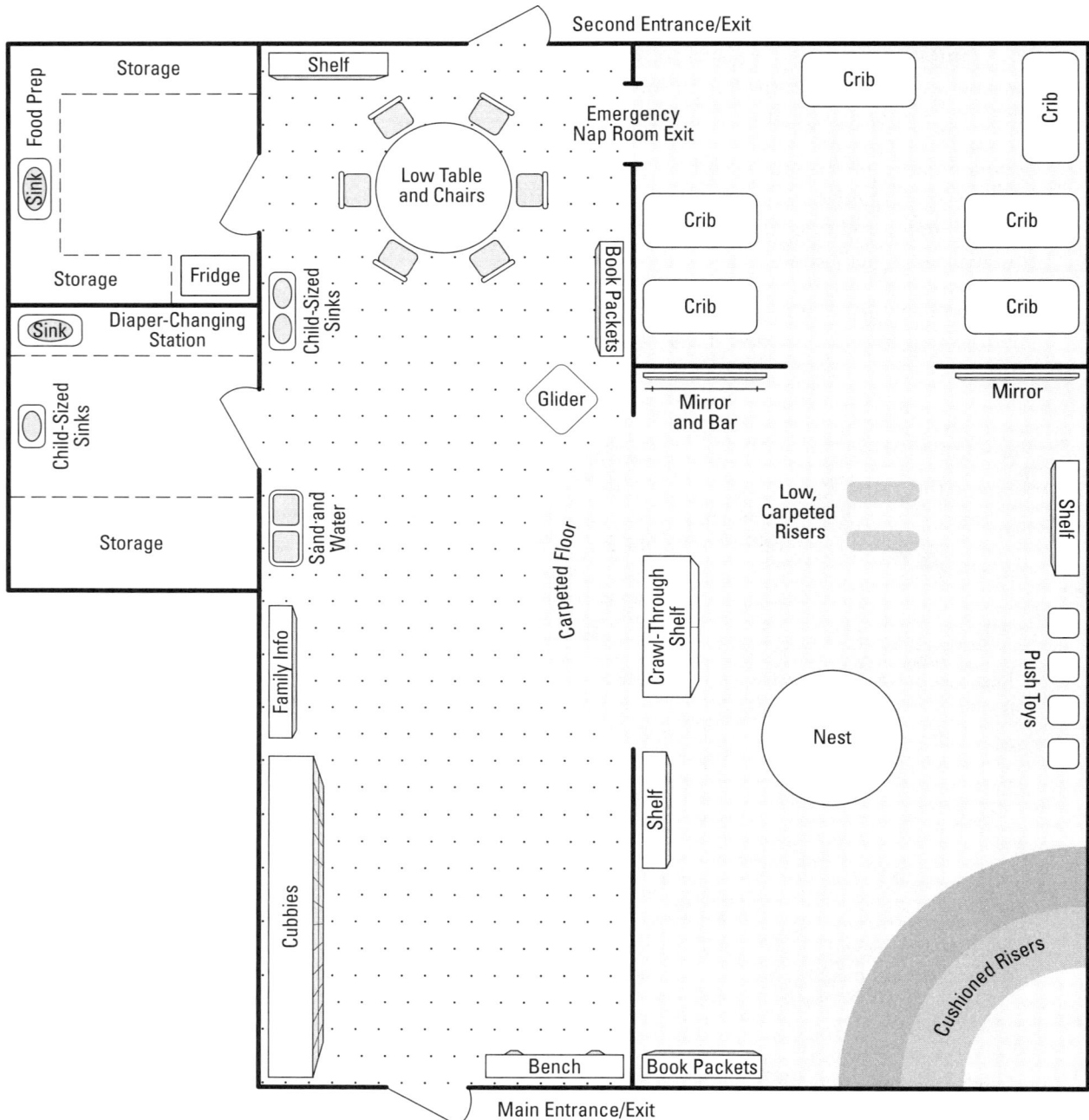

Setting Up Rooms for Toddlers and Twos

Toddlers are very active learners who change moment by moment. Sometimes they want help, but they often want to be independent. They are usually sociable, but sometimes they want to be alone. They love to move, but at times they want to be held like young infants. Their environments must be extremely rich in opportunities that support all aspects of development.

Many of the suggestions for young and mobile infant environments also apply to toddler spaces. However, some differences are necessary. Toddlers become comfortable in their use of low tables and chairs. They begin to nap on a more regular schedule, and they sleep on cots or mats rather than in cribs.

Designate a few experience areas for young toddlers and add more over the next few months. Separate noisier, more active spaces from quiet ones so that children may play freely. Remember that toddlers often gather spontaneously in larger groups when they are interested in what other children doing. Allow space for this to happen.

You can enhance toddlers' experiences by adding an increasing variety of materials and props. An indoor gross motor area, lofts or platforms, and carpeted risers help support their interest in moving and climbing. A low loft provides interesting spaces for toddlers to explore, underneath as well as on top.

Twos have additional needs. Two-year-olds usually eat together, so you need enough tables and chairs so that all of your twos can eat at the same time, although still in small groups. Define more areas for creating with art, imitating and pretending, sand and water, stories and books, playing with toys, and playing with blocks. Plan to use some of those places for music and movement and for tasting and preparing food. One of the areas should be large enough for all of the children to gather for a short time. Spaces for quiet activities, such as stories and books, should be located away from noisier activities. The increasingly complex room arrangement later helps twos make the transition to a preschool classroom.

Your decisions about the environment for toddlers and twos are based on your understanding of what they can do. The following chart lists some characteristics of toddlers and twos, and it describes ways to arrange the environment to support their development and learning.

What Toddlers and Twos Can Do	Ways You Can Arrange the Environment	How This Supports Development
Walk, run, climb, and jump	Allow space for movement and arrange equipment for safety.	Encourages toddlers to explore freely and independently
Make choices and have favorite toys	Organize toys on low shelves and label the containers and shelves with pictures and words.	Supports the development of autonomy
Eat as part of a small group	Use low tables and chairs for meals.	Helps children learn to be a member of a group and encourages conversation
Sleep at scheduled times	Provide cots or mats for napping.	Optimizes space for movement and play; allows them to get the rest they need to participate actively in the program
Sometimes want to do more than they can do	Offer materials and experiences that match children's levels of development.	Provides appropriate challenges but minimizes children's frustration
Play near and with others	Define areas where two or three children can play. Provide duplicates of toys.	Promotes children's ability to sustain social play

There are many ways to organize an environment for toddlers and twos. Use this sample layout to think about your own room.

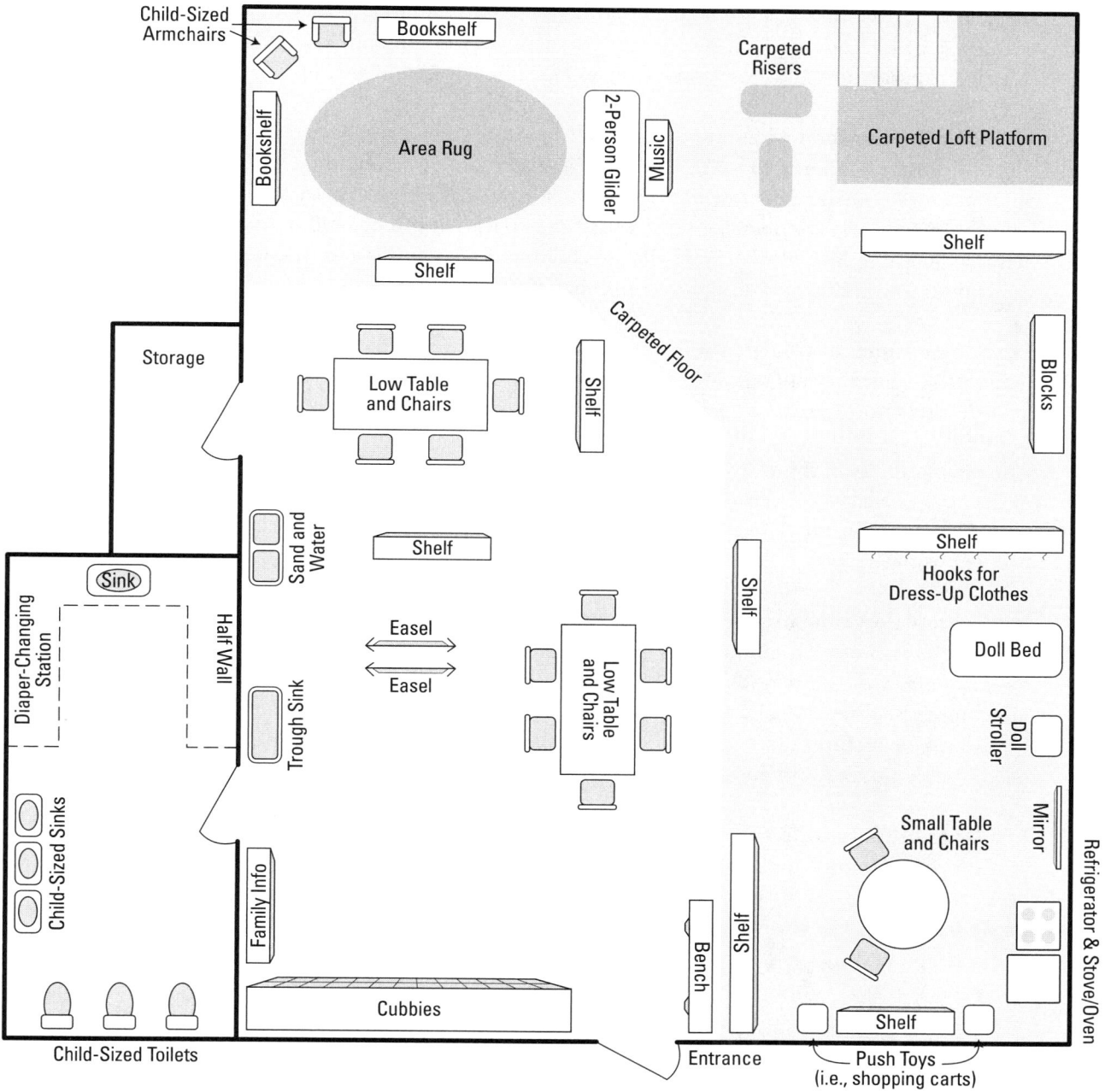

Selecting Materials

The materials you select make your environment interesting for young children to investigate. Choose materials that gently challenge children's developing abilities and skills and keep some of the familiar items that still interest them. Consider the following ideas when selecting materials.

Choose materials that promote children's development and learning. Young children learn about the world through the materials they explore during play. Include materials that encourage children to use their senses; explore shape, size, color, and balance; strengthen their muscles; experiment with cause and effect; and explore books and writing.

Include materials for a wide range of skills. Infants, toddlers, and twos grow and change quickly. Observe children to make sure that the materials you select and display are age-appropriate and challenging but not frustrating for them. Choose toys that react to children's actions. Include an assortment of open-ended materials that can be used in many different ways, such as Duplos®, blocks, and balls. As children develop skills and discover new interests, they find new ways to use familiar toys and materials.

Provide multiples of favorite toys. Young children often want to play with the same toy as their friends, but they are not developmentally ready to take turns or share. Duplicates of favorite items minimize disagreements and waiting time.

Choose materials that honor diversity. Materials should depict people similar to the children in the class as well as the diversity of society, including people with disabilities. Books, puzzles, photographs, dolls, music, art supplies, and props for imitating and pretending should portray people positively.

Incorporate homelike touches and noncommercial materials. Familiar, homelike materials remind children of their families and help them feel secure. Mobile infants, toddlers, and twos can play for long periods of time with measuring cups that nest or pots and pans with matching lids. You make toys, too. An oatmeal box and large spools can be a fill-and-dump toy. Magazine pictures can be mounted on cardboard, laminated, and cut into three pieces to make simple puzzles for twos.

Involve families in collecting materials. Ask families to help collect materials, such as pretend play props and empty appliance boxes to crawl through. Families can bring pictures for homemade books and for you to display around the room. Ask families to bring items that they would otherwise throw away, such as empty juice cans, coffee cans and lids, large spools, fabric scraps, and so forth.

Good Toys and Materials

To promote fine-motor skills

see-through rattles	clutch balls	containers to fill and dump
beanbags	busy boxes	cardboard boxes with lids
nesting cups	interlocking blocks	large beads and shoelaces
Duplos® and Bristle Blocks™	shape-sorting boxes	puzzles (3–8 pieces)

To promote gross-motor skills

riding toys	large cardboard boxes	balls of various sizes
climber and slide wagons	push-and-pull toys	low steps covered with carpet
tractor tires	tumbling mats	foam furniture covered with vinyl
	cars and trucks	

To explore with their senses

playdough	large nontoxic crayons	paper for scribbling and tearing
finger paint	sand and water table with containers and scoops	ribbons, scarves, and fabrics

To explore shape, size, color, and balance

small wooden blocks	unit blocks	rubber animals
people props	large cardboard blocks	small cars and trucks
nesting toys	foam blocks	

To encourage quiet play

tape recorder or compact disc player	cardboard and cloth books	picture books for toddlers
	blankets	soft cushions
music and story tapes and CDs		

Displaying Materials

If materials are organized and displayed thoughtfully with children's strengths and needs in mind, the children are more likely to use and care for them. Here are some suggestions for organizing and displaying toys and materials.

Store toys and related materials in the area where they will be used most often. Arrange them neatly on low shelves so children can reach them safely. Out of children's reach, store toys that are not currently in use or that need to be used with supervision.

Display toys so children can see what is available and choose what they want. Display a few carefully selected toys. An uncluttered display of carefully chosen toys is more helpful to children than crowded shelves. Offer interesting and varied toys that serve a range of abilities. Natural wood and neutral paint and surfaces make it easier for children to see brightly colored toys. Store toys with many pieces in clear plastic containers.

Use picture and word labels on containers and shelves. Labels show that everything has a place, and they help children participate in cleanup. Make labels from photographs or pictures in catalogs, or draw them on cardboard. Write labels in conventional form as the words would appear in a book. Avoid using all uppercase letters.

Rotate materials regularly. Clean and exchange materials for stored items as children outgrow or lose interest in the toys that have been displayed. In your room and in long-term storage, keep them sorted by type of toy or by the area where they will be used. This organization makes it easier to rotate toys.

Hang pictures, unbreakable mirrors, and interesting toys where children can see and touch them. Remember that eye level changes according to whether children are being held or carried, lying on a blanket on the floor, crawling around the room, or beginning to walk. Attach to the walls things that children can feel or manipulate, such as a steering wheel, beads on a wire, or boards with various textures. Mount these items either permanently or temporarily.

Special Considerations in Setting Up the Physical Environment

Think about ways to arrange the environment to address children's special requirements. First consider the need to keep children safe and healthy. In addition, think about arrangements for mixed-age groups, for children with disabilities, and for the needs of adults.

Keeping Children Safe and Healthy

Every family's primary concern is their child's safety. Your program's task is to keep children safe while allowing them to explore freely. As children develop, safety concerns change. A fully childproofed environment, designed in accordance with your knowledge of child development, can prevent or at least minimize injuries. Conduct a safety check of your indoor environment each day, and check the outdoor environment every day before the first child goes outdoors. Hazards emerge overnight. Outlet covers disappear during vacuuming. Mushrooms sprout, and litter may blow or be thrown onto the playground. Pay special attention to what is on the floor and within reach of children who are playing on the floor.

Here are some suggestions for providing a safe environment.

A Safe Environment

- Maintain appropriate staff–child ratios, and supervise all children at all times.

- Have furniture and equipment that is sized for the ages and developmental levels of the children who use the space.

- Make sure that equipment is in good repair and will not tip over. Report any equipment that needs to be repaired, and follow up to make sure it gets fixed.

- Check every day to make sure that toys are in good condition. They must not have broken parts, chipping paint, or splinters.

- Check to see that furnishings, cloth toys, bedding, and carpeting are flame resistant.

- Cover electrical outlets and use child safety locks on cupboards when appropriate.

- Keep electrical cords and electrical devices out of children's reach. Make sure that cords from window coverings are also out of children's reach.

- Check all toys and other materials to make sure that they do not present choking hazards. Remove anything with small parts. If an object can go through a choke tube or fit entirely into a child's mouth, it is too small.

- Display heavy toys on bottom shelves.

- Be sure that the water from faucets will not scald children. (It should be under 120 degrees Fahrenheit.)

- Store hazardous equipment and materials, including adult purses and tote bags, plastic bags, and cleaning supplies, out of the reach of children.

- Keep a well-stocked first-aid kit easily available and take additional kits along on walks or trips.

- Keep emergency contact information up-to-date and make sure that emergency exits are free of obstacles.

Keeping infants, toddlers, and twos healthy is another challenge. Communicable diseases cannot be eliminated, but you can minimize their spread. Keep the environment as hygienic as possible. Make sure that play spaces are clean, that bedding and soft toys are laundered, and that hard-surfaced toys are regularly cleaned and sanitized.

Frequent handwashing is critical to everyone's health. Everyone entering your program should wash his or her hands (or have them washed) before beginning work or play, as well as periodically throughout the day. Handwashing is necessary before feeding an infant, before preparing or serving food, after diapering and toileting, after touching pets, and after blowing noses. It can dramatically reduce child and adult illnesses. Post a sign to remind visitors, staff members, and families to wash their hands. Invite families to wash their hands and their children's hands as part of their good-bye routine when they arrive. It will give them something to do together to ease separation.

Here are suggestions for providing a healthy environment for infants, toddlers, and twos.

A Healthy Environment

- Wash and sanitize mouthed toys after each use. Set up a system to store mouthed toys until they can be cleaned. Set up a separate system for storing dirty laundry.

- Mix fresh bleach solutions daily. Store them within your reach at the diapering tables, eating areas, and other frequently sanitized surfaces, but keep them out of children's reach.

- Remove outdoor footwear or use shoe covers in rooms for young and mobile infants.

- Follow universal precautions and use gloves whenever blood might be present.

- Have a quiet, comfortable, supervised place for ill children to wait until their families arrive.

- Post current health news on a family bulletin board. Include information about such topics as communicable illnesses, immunizations, toy and equipment safety, and feeding.

Provide families with a copy of your health and safety policies and procedures. This shows that health and safety practices are priorities in your program.

Organizing the Environment for Mixed-Age Groups

One of the ways that programs promote continuity of care and primary caregiving is by grouping children of mixed ages. (See chapter 4, *Caring and Teaching,* for a discussion of continuity of care and primary caregiving.) Children in mixed-age groups usually remain in the same space with the same teachers over time. Here are some ideas for organizing the environment for mixed-age groups.

Keep quiet and active zones separated. Care for younger infants in protected areas, while offering mobile infants, toddlers, and twos opportunities for both quiet and very active play.

Vary the heights of tables and chairs. Review manufacturer's recommendations for children's ages and furniture heights before purchasing equipment. Look for equipment that can be adjusted to different heights.

As you choose equipment, plan for a wide range of developmental levels among the children. Both changing tables and child-size toilets are needed for mixed-age groups. Handwashing is easier when there are low sinks for toddlers and twos and sinks at a comfortable height for adults to wash young infants' hands and their own. Nap time may require cribs for younger infants, as well as small cots or mats for older infants, toddlers, and twos.

Place displays at different levels, because eye-level is different for infants who are playing on the floor, for toddlers and twos who are walking, and for children who are being held by adults.

Arrange areas where children can interact safely. A Plexiglas® panel allows children to peek at each other from either side. Mirrors that attract toddlers also interest infants. A comfortable bench or wide upholstered chair near a bookshelf will encourage a toddler to help you read a story to an infant.

Include a variety of toys and other materials that are appropriate for the developmental levels of each age group. Expect that most toys will eventually end up on the floor, and use a choke test tube to check all toys for appropriate size. Toys of a size or texture that is not good for infant play should be kept apart, for use only with teacher supervision.

Store materials for infants on lower shelves and materials for toddlers and twos on higher shelves. The lowest shelves are best for infant toys, so mobile infants can reach them from a crawling position. Children who stand can reach items on shelves at the levels of their waists and chests.

Arranging the Environment for Children With Disabilities

You may have a child with a special need or a diagnosed disability in your group. It may be a mild disability, such as a child born prematurely who uses a heart monitor when she sleeps and needs extra time to finish a bottle. Other disabilities require more complicated adaptations. For example, a child with cerebral palsy or spina bifida may need a special chair and require your help to change positions. With support from the child's family and specialists, you can adapt your environment and materials to enable the child with disabilities to participate and interact as fully as possible.

Physical Disabilities

Most of the furnishings and equipment typically found in programs for young children are appropriate for children with physical disabilities. For example, a pool of balls, soft mats to crawl on, and foam shapes to climb over are useful for children who do not have serious motor disabilities. In some instances, however, you will need to rearrange furniture and obtain adaptive equipment.

Wheel chairs or walkers—If you have a child who uses a wheelchair or walker, you may need to have some doorways widened and to install ramps and grab bars. Some simple environmental changes include rearranging tables or play areas to provide space to maneuver special equipment. Make sure your program's outdoor environment is also arranged for wheelchairs and walkers.

Support for sitting and standing—To participate fully in the program, some children with physical disabilities need physical support when they sit and stand. A large cushion can be shaped to provide support for sitting. Several types of specialized chairs are also available. *Educube®* chairs are hard chairs with a raised back and sides. *Tumbleform* chairs are firm foam chairs in various sizes, and *pummel* chairs have a knob between the spaces for children's legs. Other therapeutic chairs and prone standers, which provide support for the child's trunk and lower body, are designed and manufactured specifically for a child's size and special need.

Help in changing positions—Some children with physical disabilities need help to change their positions. They need assistance to stay comfortable and to be able to explore their environments. Family members and physical or occupational therapists working with the child can show you the best positions for different kinds of play. Positioning children with physical disabilities might require bolsters, wedges, or other positioning tools, along with chairs and prone standers. Positioning equipment should be kept near experience areas so that the child can change activities easily. In classroom displays, include photographs of children with motor impairments who are positioned comfortably for play. The photos will help visiting adults and substitute teachers as they interact with the children.

Sensory Impairments

Sensory problems include visual impairment and blindness, hearing impairment and deafness, and sensory integration disorders. Children with sensory impairments need clear cues the encourage them to use their strengths. Children with sensory integration disorders need environments in which sensory stimulation can be adjusted.

Children with **visual impairments** learn to pay attention to the information they receive by listening, touching, smelling, and tasting. The sounds of music and familiar voices are reassuring. Clear pathways and well-defined areas help them move from place to place. Textural cues, such as change of texture from carpet to tile, help children know that they have entered a different part of the room. A piece of material such as felt or fur can help children with visual impairments find their cubbies.

Children with **hearing impairments** use visual cues, touch, vibration, tastes, and smells to interpret what is happening around them. Good acoustics and minimal conflicting noise help children who have at least some hearing. Since these children rely heavily on visual information, make sure that the inside lighting is adequate and free of glare. Play areas that encourage face-to-face interactions help children with hearing impairments read the facial cues of their playmates.

Some children with physical and developmental disabilities have **tactile defensiveness**, which causes them to avoid directly touching some materials, such as paint, water, or playdough. Provide gloves, sticks, paint brushes, and other tools and props to encourage them to participate in sensory activities as they choose.

Meeting the Needs of Adults for Comfort

Caring for young children is a physically challenging job. Rather than forcing yourself to do physically difficult tasks, make them easier by using techniques such as these.

Minimize physical strain whenever possible. Place resilient cushioned mats in front of the diapering table and other places where adults stand a great deal. A small armrest pillow reduces strain when bottle-feeding infants. When working with mobile infants, low carpeted risers and cubes for adult seating help you observe, join floor play, and stand up easily. Steps for children to climb to the diapering table limit your need to lift them. Toddlers and twos can push low chairs to the table, assist with wiping tables with soapy water after meals, and pick up some toys. Keep a small dustpan and broom nearby so you can pick up toys from the floor without bending. Provide several kinds of comfortable adult seating as well.

Well-organized storage areas help you find things easily and enable you to remain attentive to the children. Adults also need places to store their personal belongings out of children's reach. Purses, bags, and coat pockets are filled with fascinating things that are sometimes dangerous for young children. You need spaces to store extra children's clothing, medications if they are stored in the room, and materials that are not currently in use.

Sending Positive Messages

Have you ever watched children and their family members when they first visit your room? They look around to decide what kind of place it is. They may be wondering:

- Do I belong here?
- Do these people know who I am? Do they like me?
- Is this a place I can trust?
- Will I be safe here?
- Will I be comfortable here?
- Can I move around and explore?
- Is this a calm and interesting place to be?
- Can I count on these people to take care of me?

Because you are the most important part of the learning environment, your daily interactions with infants, toddlers, and twos are the most important way to answer these concerns. Your arrangement of the physical environment also sends powerful messages to children and their families. Think about whether it conveys the messages you intend.

You belong here. We like you.

- At children's eye levels, display photos of the children at play and with their families. Change them occasionally. Laminate them or use a Plexiglas® cover so children can touch them without tearing them. Put photos in unbreakable cube frames that children may carry around.
- Provide places for each child to store belongings from home.
- Make sure that pictures and materials honor the ethnic and individual characteristics of the children and families.
- Change the environment on the basis of your observations of children. For example, when children begin to climb on the bookshelf, add large cushions or plastic boxes that children may climb on instead.
- Encourage family members to bring interesting materials for children to explore, such as colorful bandanas, stackable bottle caps, or a guitar.

This is a place you can trust. You will be safe here.

- Arrange the furniture with safety in mind. Cushion surfaces where children are learning to move on their own, making sure that the cushioning does not interfere with balance.
- Store items near the places where they will be used. Label containers, cupboards, and shelves so that substitute teachers, adult visitors, and family members can find things easily.
- Limit environmental changes to help cautious children know that they can depend on the room arrangement.

This is a comfortable place to be.

- Include homelike touches and familiar household objects in the environment, such as curtains, large floor cushions, nontoxic plants, and even plastic tumblers to stack.
- Make sure that children's comfort items are available to them.
- Provide soft furniture, such as stuffed chairs and couches.
- Have enough space for teachers and family members to join children in their play.
- Place reading materials in many places around the room so children and adults may sit and enjoy them.
- Use soft textures and furnishings to help moderate noisy sounds. Soft colors, lights, and sounds foster a peaceful atmosphere.

You can move freely and explore on your own.
- Set aside sufficient space so that children can turn over, crawl, creep, pull up, stand, cruise, and walk around as they grow and change. Borrow this space from other areas when necessary. For instance, you can push cribs closer together temporarily, to leave more floor space when children are not napping.
- Block off areas that are unsafe for children.
- Store a variety of materials on shelves that are low enough for children to reach.
- Make sure that all of the materials stored or set out on low shelves are intended for children's use.
- Label shelves and containers with pictures and words so children know where to find and return materials.
- Display toys, books, and other materials in consistent places so children know where to find them.
- Designate areas for experiences as children's strengths, needs, and interests change.

We will take care of you.
- Set up areas for routines.
- Designate a crib, cot, or mat for each child.
- Provide a comfortable, supervised place where sick children may rest until their parents come.

Scan your room regularly to look for ways the environment can be enhanced to convey these positive messages. Small, special touches make the environment warm and welcoming to everyone: children, families, and you.

Creating a Structure for Each Day

Structure is the second aspect of creating a responsive environment for infants, toddlers, and twos. A predictable sequence of events enables children, their families, and you to feel a sense of order. While your daily schedule and plans need to be flexible, they give you direction for your work with children.

Planning a Daily Schedule

Infants, toddlers, and twos need a schedule that is regular enough to be predictable but flexible enough to meet their individual needs and to take advantage of the learning opportunities that emerge continually every day. In general, the younger the children, the more flexible and individualized the schedule must be. Yet even babies feel more secure when the schedule is somewhat consistent. Responsive care respects children's biological rhythms and their interests.

When an infant falls asleep soon after arriving at child care, she needs a nap even though the other children are awake and playing. When the wind begins swirling leaves in the backyard, 2-year-olds might want to play outside even though the schedule suggests that it is time to come inside for lunch.

Parts of a Daily Schedule

When you create a daily schedule, remember to allow adequate time for these routines:

- hellos and good-byes
- diapering and toileting
- eating and mealtimes
- sleeping and nap time
- dressing

These routines are discussed in depth in chapters 6–10.

In addition to providing routine care, you plan experiences that promote children's development and learning. These include

- playing with toys
- imitating and pretending
- enjoying stories and books
- connecting with music and movement
- creating with art
- tasting and preparing food
- exploring sand and water
- exploring outdoors

These experiences are discussed in chapters 11–18. Your task is to create daily schedules that include routines and a variety of experiences when individual children and small groups are ready for them.

Characteristics of an Appropriate Schedule

- The schedule is flexible and adaptable. It is changed to meet individual needs.
- The schedule sets an unhurried, child-directed pace for the routines and experiences of the day.
- There is sufficient time for routines, play experiences, and transitions.
- There is a balance between active and quiet times.
- Children have opportunities to be alone (although supervised) or with a familiar teacher.
- Children have opportunities to spend time in small groups of 2–3 children.
- Children go outdoors twice a day in full-day programs.

The schedule you develop for your program may vary from those outlined. However, the sample schedules that are suggested here will give you ideas for planning a schedule that meets the needs of your children and your program.

Individualizing the Schedule for Infants

Each child in your care has his or her own schedule for eating, diapering and toileting, playing, and sleeping. In an infant room, each infant is fed when hungry, sleeps in a familiar place when tired, and has his or her diaper changed when it is wet or soiled. With adult help, infants begin to develop their own patterns for sleeping, eating, and other basic needs, but each has his own schedule. In an infant room, there are as many schedules as there are infants.

The next chart shows the sequence of events during one day in the lives of two infants, Julio (4 months) and Willard (11 months). Notice that, although they do many of the same activities, the timing and specific content of what they do differ.

Julio's Day

Morning

Arrival: Julio arrives with his mother. She takes a while to say good-bye and gives Julio to Linda.

Mealtime: Julio sits in a glider with Linda. She cradles him in her arm as she gives him a bottle.

Diaper change: Julio gazes at Linda as she changes his diaper and talks to him. He begins rubbing his eyes.

Nap time: Julio falls asleep in his crib after Linda pats him gently and softly sings a lullaby.

Diaper change: Julio's diaper is dry when Linda checks it.

Indoor play: Julio lies on a mat with two other babies near a low, shatterproof mirror. Linda sits at the edge of the mat and talks with the three children about what they are seeing and doing.

Mealtime: Julio drinks part of a bottle while he sits on Linda's lap. Then he burps as Linda gently pats his back.

Diaper change: Julio kicks his legs as Linda changes his diaper. "You're kicking your legs," she explains. "I'm going to put your pants back on those legs now."

Dressing: Linda puts on Julio's jacket. She sings to him as she dresses him.

Outdoor play: Linda takes Julio outdoors, walking around the playground with him. He closes his eyes when a gust of wind blows across his face. Linda tells him that the moving air he feels on his face is wind.

Willard's Day

Morning

Arrival: Willard arrives at the center with his mother. Willard cries as his mother says good-bye. Grace comforts him by reading a book with him.

Mealtime: Grace helps Willard wash his hands to get ready for breakfast. He sits in a small sturdy chair at a low table. He feeds himself the apple slices on his plate and drinks milk from a training cup. After breakfast, he swipes his hands with a wet paper towel, and then Grace helps him wash them more thoroughly.

Indoor play: Willard squeezes, pounds, and pokes a soft squeaky toy. He looks at Grace and laughs with delight each time the toy squeaks.

Diaper change: Grace changes Willard's diaper, naming body parts as she touches them.

Indoor play: Grace sings with Willard and two other children. Willard notices his family picture album, picks it up, and turns the pages. He points to his mother's picture when Grace asks, "Where's Mommy?"

Diaper change: Willard protests as Grace picks him up to change his diaper. Grace assures him that it will only take a minute. He lies still and helps open the diaper tabs.

Dressing: Willard takes his jacket off its hook. Grace helps him put it on.

Outdoor play: Grace spreads a big blanket near the fence and puts Willard on the blanket. He pulls to standing by holding onto the fence. He points to cars, dogs, and people as they pass by.

Julio's Day

Midday

Diaper change: Linda changes Julio, focusing on him but remaining attentive to the other children.

Mealtime: Linda puts Julio on her lap and offers him his bottle. He turns his head away, indicating that he is not ready to eat just now. She tries again in 10 minutes. He is hungry and drinks his bottle.

Nap time: Julio begins dozing off. Linda puts him on his back in his crib and gently pats his tummy a few times before letting him fall asleep on his own.

Diaper change: Linda talks quietly to Julio as she changes his diaper. They enjoy a game of peek-a-boo together.

Mealtime: Julio drinks part of a bottle while Linda cradles him on her lap.

Afternoon

Indoor play: Julio sits on Linda's lap as she sings with older infants.

Diaper change: Linda notices that Julio is wet and changes his diaper. He squirms, so she talks to him calmly and finishes quickly.

Indoor play: Linda places Julio under a play gym on a floor mat. Julio bats the objects on the gym with his fist.

Dressing: Linda puts Julio's jacket on again.

Outdoor play: Linda carries Julio outside. She sings "Ring Around a Rosie," and Julio laughs every time she stoops as she sings, "All fall down!"

Departure: Julio sits on a glider with his mother while she relaxes and talks with Linda. After about 10 minutes, she puts on Julio's jacket, says good-bye, and they leave for home.

Willard's Day

Midday

Diaper change/handwashing: Willard's diaper is dry when Grace checks it. With Grace's help, Willard washes his hands

Mealtime: Willard sits at a low table with Grace and three other children. He takes the spoon from Grace and tries to feed himself applesauce. Grace laughs and asks, "Willard, are you feeding yourself or the table?" After lunch, Grace helps Willard wash his hands, and she brushes his teeth.

Diaper change: Willard yawns and lies quietly as Grace changes his diaper.

Nap time: Willard falls asleep almost instantly when Grace puts him in his crib. After sleeping for about an hour, Willard begins to make quiet sounds in his crib.

Diaper change: Grace checks Willard's diaper and changes it, singing one of his favorite songs.

Snack: Willard drinks formula from a training cup and eats some pear slices with his fingers.

Afternoon

Indoor play: Willard pushes a plastic crate around the room, stopping repeatedly to put things into it, dump them out, and fill the box again.

Cleanup: Grace encourages Willard to help put the balls back in the basket. She takes turns with him to make it into a game.

Diaper change: Willard's diaper is wet when Grace checks it. Before picking him up, she explains, "Okay, let's change this wet diaper."

Dressing: Willard squirms as Grace helps him put on his jacket. "Willard, here's your hat," Grace says. "Please put it on your head while I put on your jacket."

Outdoor play: Willard sits in the sandbox, filling and dumping a bucket of wet sand.

Departure: Willard exclaims, "Da-da!" when he hears his father's voice. He takes two steps toward his father and then crawls over, sits, holds his arms up, and smiles as his father picks him up.

The Individual Care Plan you develop with each family will enable you to create a personal schedule for each infant (see chapter 5, "Partnering With Families"). Janet completed the "Individual Care Plan" form for Jasmine (8 months) after her conversation with the Jones family.

Individual Care Plan

Child: Jasmine
Child's Date of Birth: Infants
Teacher: Janet & Tamika
Family Member(s): Donna & Lee Jones
Date: March 25, 2010

Arrival

Jasmine arrives by 7:30. Dad usually brings her.

Eating

Jasmine eats jarred baby food that her family provides. She also eats some finger foods: Cheerios®, bread, bananas, peaches, and very tender potatoes and carrots. She has a bottle before she naps. She usually eats lunch after she wakes up from her nap at around 11:30 and has an afternoon snack around 3:30.

Diapering

Jasmine usually needs her diaper changed about 30–45 minutes after eating. She likes to be actively involved and enjoys playing with her toes and fingers during diapering.

Dressing

Jasmine has a couple of extra sets of clothes in her cubby. It is important that she be in a clean outfit when her grandma picks her up in the afternoon.

Sleeping

Jasmine takes two naps, one from 10:00–11:30 and another from 2:30–3:30. She likes to have her back rubbed before her morning nap, and she is used to hearing a song before her afternoon nap.

Departure

Jasmine's grandma usually picks her up by 4:30.

Once you have completed the "Individual Care Plan" form for each of the infants in your primary care group, you can develop an overall schedule for your group that shows the approximate times of the daily routines for each child. The actual times will change from day to day, but a general routines schedule will help you and your co-teachers coordinate responsibilities. The routines schedule will also help you decide when to provide experiences for children who are awake but not eating or having their diapers changed. You will also have an idea about when to schedule morning and afternoon outdoor times.

Schedules for Toddlers and Twos

By the time children are toddlers, their days are more consistent and group-oriented. For example, toddlers and twos typically eat and sleep as a group and have designated times for playing. A consistent daily schedule helps them feel more in control and thus more competent and secure. It is still important to be flexible about responding to individual children's needs and to maintain an unhurried pace each day.

Here is a sample schedule for toddlers who are enrolled in a full-day program. Notice that several activities often take place at the same time. The actual times on your schedule may vary, depending upon your children's needs.

DAILY SCHEDULE

7:00–8:30 **Planning/preparation time:** Review the plans for the day. Conduct health and safety checks. Refill bathroom and diaper changing supplies. Make bleach solution. Set out materials for children to use as they arrive. Think about individual children and any special needs.

Hellos and good-byes: As children transition from home to school, greet each child and help them say good-bye to each other.

Dressing: Help children take off and store their outerwear.

Diapering and toileting: Check diapers and change as necessary. Take older children to the toilet as needed.

Eating and mealtimes: Help children wash hands and eat breakfast. Sit with children and enjoy breakfast together. Wash hands and brush teeth.

8:30–10:15 **Indoor Play:** Guide children in selecting what they want to play with and how. Observe and interact with children to extend play and learning. Find time to read to children individually or in a very small group.

Diapering and toileting: Check diapers and change as necessary. Take older children to the toilet as needed.

Sleeping and nap time: Allow tired children to sleep according to their needs, even if they usually sleep at the same time as the rest of the group.

Dressing: Change children's wet or soiled clothing as necessary.

Cleanup: Help children put materials away.

Eating and mealtimes: Help children wash hands and eat morning snack. Sit with children and enjoy a snack and conversation together.

10:15–11:30 **Dressing:** Help children put on outerwear before going outdoors.

Outdoor play: Supervise and interact with children as they explore the playground environment and equipment. Roll balls back and forth, blow bubbles, paint with water, make natural discoveries, and so on.

Dressing: Help children take off and store their outerwear.

DAILY SCHEDULE, *continued*

11:30–12:30 **Diapering and toileting:** Check diapers and change as necessary. Take older children to the toilet as needed.

Eating and mealtimes: Help children wash hands and eat lunch. Sit with children and encourage conversation about the day's events, the meal itself, and other things of interest to the children. Wash hands and faces; brush teeth.

12:30–2:30 **Sleeping and nap time:** Help children relax so they can fall asleep. Supervise napping children, sharing duties so each teacher gets a break. Provide quiet activities for children who do not sleep. Adjust length of nap time to suit the group pattern and the needs of individual children.

2:30–3:00 **Diapering and toileting:** Check diapers as children awaken and change as needed. Take older children to the toilet.

Eating and mealtimes: Set up snack so children can eat as they wake up.

3:00–4:00 **Experiences:** Guide children in selecting what they want to play with and how. Observe and interact with children to extend play and learning. Read and sing with children individually or in a small group.

4:00–5:00 **Dressing:** Help children put on outerwear before going outdoors.

Outdoor play: Use outdoor playground or take children on walks.

Dressing: Help children take off and store their outerwear.

5:00–6:00 **Experiences:** Set out a limited number of choices for children so they are engaged until their parents arrive. Read stories to a child or a small group of children.

Diapering and toileting: Check diapers and change as needed. Take older children to the toilet.

Dressing: Send home wet or soiled clothing and bedding.

Hellos and good-byes: Help children and families reconnect at the end of the day. Greet each parent and share something special about their child's day.

As time allows during the day **Planning and reflection:** Discuss with colleagues how the day went and what you observed about individual children's needs, interests, and accomplishments. Make plans for the next day.

Adapting the Daily Schedule for 2-Year-Olds

Twos can engage in more extended play. They are also ready to sit with a small group of 2–4 children during a planned story time. Here are some things to keep in mind when planning a schedule for this age group:

- Include active and quiet times.
- Schedule time for outdoor play in the morning and in the afternoon.
- Be aware of children's individual needs for sleeping, eating, and toileting.
- Keep group times short. Allow children to decide how long they want to stay with the group. Be ready to stop when you see that most children are losing interest.
- Display your schedule at children's eye level, illustrated with drawings or photographs of scheduled activities.
- Plan for transitions.

Planning for Transitions

Every day is filled with transitions, the periods between one routine or experience and the next. Transitions are more apparent for toddlers and twos than for infants, because the older children have a more structured schedule. The most important transitions, and often most difficult, are at the beginning and end of the day. (This is discussed in detail in chapter 6, "Hellos and Good-Byes".) However, any transition can be a problem if children do not know what to do or if they are required to wait too long. To avoid disruptive behavior, always give children something to do while they are waiting.

Here are some suggestions for preparing for transitions.

Plan ahead. Thinking and organizing supplies ahead of time allows you to give the children your full attention.

Be organized. Have the supplies for the next activity ready so you do not have to search for them while the children wait.

Give children a warning. Before a change takes place, tell them that it is coming. For example, before cleaning up toys and washing hands for lunch, you might say, "It's almost time to clean up. Finish what you are doing, and then we will help each other put the toys away. It is almost time for lunch."

Give clear directions. Make sure your instructions are appropriate for the developmental level of the child. For example, a child who can only follow one-step directions will be confused if you tell him to put the balls in the shed, go inside, hang up his coat, and wash his hands.

Avoid having children wait. Divide the group so children will not have to wait. For example, while some 2-year-olds are brushing their teeth, the others might be listening to a story or helping you put blankets on cots.

Guide children through transitions. Do this by describing what you are doing or by singing or chanting together. For example, you can have a special song for clean-up time or for getting ready for lunch.

Planned transitions help children build a sense of order. They feel competent when they know what is expected and when they are engaged. A well-organized day will help you remain calm and allow you to observe children and enjoy their development.

Responsive Planning

The importance of building responsive relationships is emphasized throughout *The Creative Curriculum*®. Teachers must observe children purposefully, think about what they learn about each child, and respond in supportive ways. Even though you develop a plan for each day, you must always be open to following children's interests and addressing their needs.

As you care for and teach infants, toddlers, and twos, you balance planning—thinking ahead about what you might do during a week or a day—with following the child's lead at particular moments. You need to know when to watch, when to step in, and how to extend each child's learning. When you know individual children's interests and developmental levels, you can offer experiences that engage and delight children and build their competence. Children feel understood and thrive in your care when their individual needs are met.

Using Observations to Respond to and Plan for Each Child

As you work with infants, toddlers, and twos, you continually observe what they are doing and saying. Refer to *Objectives for Development & Learning* as you observe children. Think about what you see and hear and determine how to respond at the moment. Later, you can use your observation notes to complete weekly planning forms. Ongoing observation will help you shape daily routines and experiences and continually enhance your relationship with each child. In chapters 11–18, you will see examples of how teachers observe children at different points during the day, what they think about, how they respond at the moment, and their ideas for incorporating the information into their weekly plans.

Using the Weekly Planning Forms

To help you prepare for each day and still respond to children's changing interests and abilities, *The Creative Curriculum*® includes two weekly planning forms: the "Child Planning Form" and the "Group Planning Form."

The "Child Planning Form" is used on a weekly basis to record current information about each child. It helps you use what you know about each child to plan experiences that support his development and learning. This enables you individualize your program.

To offer a program that meets each child's needs, you need to know and appreciate what makes each child unique. When you understand what motivates a child, how the child approaches new tasks, and his preferred learning style, you can plan for him. The "Child Planning Form" helps you do this. Each week, take a few minutes to review your observation notes, examine portfolio samples, think about recent events and interactions, and analyze the information you have about each child in your primary care group. Record the most important facts in the "Current Information" section. Then note how you will use this information in the coming week. For example, describe changes you might make to routines and list materials you might introduce to the child.

This is how Brooks completed the "Child Planning Form" for the four children in her group.

Child Planning Form

Teacher(s):	Brooks
Group:	Infants
Week of:	February 2–6

Child: Abby (14 months)

Current information:
Abby has been filling purses with small toys and carrying them around. She's also starting to nap earlier in the morning.

Plans:
Add some small baskets to the room for filling and carrying. Adjust the schedule to accommodate her new nap time.

Child: Max (16 months)

Current information:
Max played with two simple puzzles every day.

Plans:
Add two new knob puzzles and leave the old ones. Encourage him to discover and try the new ones.

Child: Devon (18 months)

Current information:
Devon enjoyed hearing *The Itsy-Bitsy Spider* board book. He's started to do the hand motions.

Plans:
Continue reading the book. Bring the spider puppet to use with the book.

Child: Shawntee (18 months)

Current information:
Shawntee needs to be by me when new adults are around.

Plans:
Make sure I'm available to her on Friday when Max's dad comes to volunteer.

The "Group Planning Form" helps you think about all of the children in your group and decide what changes to make to the environment, general schedule, and routines. It also helps you decide what experiences to offer during the week. It gives you an overall sense of direction for the week and a list of the materials you want to have available.

Think about weekly planning as *planning for possibilities.* You prepare for routines and meaningful experiences and then follow each child's lead. Infants, toddlers, and twos often respond in unexpected ways to new materials and to planned experiences. Observing and responding to what children do each day is one of the joys of working with young children. If your plans are flexible and you feel free to revise them as often as you think best, you are more likely to take advantage of learning opportunities that arise during the course of daily life in the program. To complete the "Group Planning Form," think about the following questions:

- What experiences interest the children now?
- Which materials are the children using most?
- What skills are children developing?
- What is working well? What is not working well?
- How are we providing meaningful roles for family members who visit the program?

Your answers to these questions will help you make decisions about your program. The "Group Planning Form" includes five main sections.

Changes to the environment—Record the changes you will make to the environment next week. Your observations guide the changes. For example, if puzzle pieces were often scattered on the floor, you might decide that the puzzles are too difficult and should be put away for now. Perhaps you will decide that the puzzles are not stored so that children can use them independently, and you might decide to put them on a lower shelf. If a child shows a particular interest in playing with a ball, you might decide to include balls of different sizes in the play area. Perhaps it is time to add new labels to the shelves to help toddlers clean up after themselves. You might plan to rotate toys that children have not played with for a while, replacing them with different toys that capture children's interest.

Changes to routines and schedule—Record the ways you will change routines next week. For example, if a child has been having trouble going to sleep, organize his sleeping routine so you can rock him until he is drowsy. If a child is too hungry before lunch time, you might offer lunch earlier or find ways to eliminate waiting when it is time for the meal. If you and a toddler's parents agree that it is time to begin toilet learning, note that on the "Group Planning Form."

Family involvement—Include your ideas about involving family members next week. These may include asking for their help in making materials and inviting them to participate in an experience or in daily routines.

Special experiences I plan to offer this week—Enter experiences you will offer to support children's exploration and discoveries. Think about the experiences you can provide indoors and outdoors. Remember to give children opportunities to choose what they want to do and the people with whom to play. Chapters 11–18 discuss experiences. You do not have to plan a different experience every day or offer every kind of experience every day. Infants, toddlers, and twos master skills through repetition, and they take delight in repeating the same thing again and again.

Thoughts for next week—Complete this section when you think about your current week. Include information about how engaged the children were. Did one child roll balls down a ramp for 20 minutes? Were other children involved? Think about what actually happened and about any changes you want to make for the following week. For example, do you want to add more balls or balls of different sizes? Perhaps you want to see what happens if you add a large inclined tube for the children to roll balls down, instead of a ramp.

Here is an example of the "Group Planning Form" that Brooks completed by using the information from the "Child Planning Form."

TeachingStrategies®

Group Planning Form

Teacher(s):	Brooks
Group:	Infants
Week of:	February 2–6

Changes to the Environment:
  Add a variety of small baskets (plastic and wicker) for filling and carrying.
  Put out two new knob puzzles next to the familiar ones.
  Put the spider puppet in the book area. Look for a CD with the "*Itsy-Bitsy Spider.*"

Changes to Routines and Schedule:
  Start going outside 15 minutes earlier in the morning, to accommodate new nap times.

Family Involvement:
  Max's dad is coming for the morning on Friday.

Special Experiences I Plan to Offer This Week					
	Monday	**Tuesday**	**Wednesday**	**Thursday**	**Friday**
Indoor Experiences	Read *The Itsy-Bitsy Spider* and use the puppet (all week)	Water play inside (small tubs with water and pouring cups)	Water play inside (small tubs with water and pouring cups)	Get ready for the picnic—help pack the picnic basket	Max's dad visits for the morning
Outdoor Experiences	Introduce the new climber	Use the new climber	Use the new climber	Morning picnic on the	Walk to the park

Volume 1: The Foundation

Chapter 2: **Creating a Responsive Environment**

Planning for Twos

Sometimes you may notice that many 2-year-olds are interested in the same topic. You might want to expand on their interest by incorporating several different experiences related to the topic into your weekly plans. In order to do this, you need to consider their developmental skills as well as their interests.

LaToya and her assistant teacher looked at their observation notes from the week as they prepared to write next week's plans. They had several notes about children who discovered and collected leaves on the playground. Abraham, Jonisha, Marcus, Valisha, Donovan, Josie, and Annemarie were interested in the leaves. Jonisha, Marcus, and Abraham had asked why the leaves fell off the tree. Another note said that Donovan and Josie chased leaves as they fell from the trees, jumping to try to catch them. In considering what they might do to encourage the children's interest in leaves, they also thought about the children's skills. They knew that the children can

- sit in a small group and listen to a short story
- group objects that have similar characteristics
- use writing and painting tools such as crayons and paint brushes
- use language to describe objects

LaToya wondered, "How I can I extend the children's learning?" After discussing their ideas, LaToya and her assistant decided to include the exploration of leaves in their plans. They agreed to observe the children's level of interest this coming week to decide whether they should continue the exploration of leaves for the following week or two. Here are their ideas for experiences:

Books: *Red Leaf, Yellow Leaf*, by Lois Ehlert; *Look What I Did With a Leaf*, by Morteza Sohi; *A Tree is Nice*, by Marc Simon; *Leaf Man*, by Lois Ehlert; *A Simple Brown Leaf*, by L. J. Davis

Encourage the children to collect leaves on the playground to examine inside.

Take a walk around the neighborhood and look at and collect other leaves.

Bring magnifying glasses outside to examine leaves there.

Talk about the sizes, shapes, and colors of the leaves and ask questions:

- What do they feel like?
- What do they look like?

Put paint of the colors of the leaves at two art easels outside.

Creative movement inside (moving like leaves falling from the trees).

Provide crayons without wrappings and thin paper for leaf rubbings.

Sort the leaves into simple categories (same color, big/little).

Add leaves to the collage materials in the art area.

Bring child-sized rakes outside.

Here is the "Child Planning Form" that LaToya completed for her group after observing the children.

Child Planning Form

Teacher(s):	LaToya
Group:	Twos
Week of:	November 4–8

Child: Samuel

Current information:
Had two toileting accidents this week during outdoor play.

Plans:
Halfway through outdoor time, remind him to use the bathroom.

Child: Valisha

Current information:
Collected leaves on the playground with Annemarie.

Plans:
Bring baskets outside for the children to use for gathering leaves.

Child: Donovan

Current information:
His aunt and baby cousin have moved in with his family.

Plans:
Continue to observe Donovan for changes in his behavior. Talk with him about what it is like to have a baby in his house. Continue to talk with his mom at drop-off time.

Child: Jonisha

Current information:
Pretended to read books to two children in the library. Asked questions about leaves on the playground.

Plans:
Add some books about leaves to the library and read them with Jonisha.

Child: Marcus

Current information:
Painted with water on the playground, three days in a row.

Plans:
Set up easels and paint outside.

Child: Josie

Current information:
Chased leaves on the playground with Donovan.

Plans:
Bring in streamers and encourage Josie to move like falling leaves.

Here is the "Group Planning Form" that LaToya completed for her group after the brainstorming session.

Group Planning Form

Teacher(s):	LaToya
Group:	Twos
Week of:	November 4–8

Changes to the Environment:

Bring baskets outside for leaves gathered on the playground.
Add easel to the playground.
Introduce magnifying glasses.

Changes to Routines and Schedule:

Remind children during outdoor play to use the bathroom.

Family Involvement:

Ask for volunteers to go on a walking trip around the neighborhood.

Special Experiences I Plan to Offer This Week					
	Monday	**Tuesday**	**Wednesday**	**Thursday**	**Friday**
Indoor Experiences	Music & Movement: move like leaves Read *Red Leaf, Yellow Leaf* and discuss leaves on playground	Read *Red Leaf, Yellow Leaf* and discuss the colors of the leaves on the playground	Read *A Simple Brown Leaf* Use magnifying glasses to look at leaves at the sensory table	Read *A Tree is Nice* Use magnifying glasses to look at leaves at the sensory table	Prepare for the walking trip
Outdoor Experiences	Collecting leaves on the playground	Easel Painting	Easel Painting Raking leaves	Raking leaves	Walking trip around the neighborhood to look at and collect leaves

Adapting Your Plans

When you work with children from birth to age 3, you must always expect the unexpected. Each infant has a personal schedule and style. As you zip the last jacket and head for the door, an infant may begin crying to tell you he is tired or hungry or needs his diaper changed. Toddlers and twos also have an amazing ability to capsize the best-laid plans. You cannot be sure about when a toddler will decide to flush her socks down the toilet or try to feed his leftover lunch to his teddy bear.

Remember, being responsive is more important than sticking to your plan. Always keep in mind that your positive interactions with children are more important than particular activities. You will need to adapt your plans as you respond to the children's changing needs and interests. Here are some steps to follow.

Review your weekly planning forms. Think about the day before the children arrive. Try to imagine how all the parts of the day will fit together.

Assess the realities of the day. Will an infant need extra time and attention because she is teething? Did a family bring in a bag of freshly picked apples, tempting you to make applesauce for a snack? Are you feeling a little tired and not up to taking the walk you planned?

Remain flexible and adapt your plans as necessary. No matter how carefully you prepare, you must always be ready to change your plans. For example, a toddler might throw a tantrum and need some extra attention, requiring you to postpone the large chalk activity you had planned. Perhaps a bulldozer will begin working at the end of your road, giving you a new purpose for neighborhood walks.

Be responsive to individual children's needs and interests. For example, if you know a child needs you to be ready to step in to keep her from biting another child, you might decide to postpone your plans for making playdough with the children. Instead, you would bring out the playdough you made a few days ago or spend extra time singing and reading with the children. You can make new playdough tomorrow or next week.

Conclusion

This chapter discussed the second component of *The Creative Curriculum® for Infants, Toddlers & Twos:* creating a responsive environment. It explained how the physical environment promotes the developing abilities and interests of infants, toddlers, and twos; how the environment supports responsive relationships; and how to plan a structure that gives you direction but allows flexibility. When you thoughtfully organize your room and plan for each child, you create a responsive environment in which children can flourish and learn. The learning component of the curriculum is discussed in the next chapter, "What Children Are Learning."

What Children Are Learning

The Foundation for All Learning	80
Building Language and Literacy Skills	81
Vocabulary and Language	81
The Sounds and Rhythms of Language	83
Enjoying Books and Stories	85
Exploring Writing	87
Promoting Language and Literacy Learning	89
Discovering Mathematical Relationships	92
Number Concepts	92
Patterns and Relationships	93
Geometry and Spatial Relationships	94
Sorting and Classifying	95
Helping Children Discover Mathematical Relationships	96
Exploring Like Scientists	98
The Physical World	98
The Natural World	99
The Social World	100
Encouraging Children to Explore Like Scientists	101

What Children Are Learning

Watch an infant, toddler, or 2-year-old interacting with others or exploring the environment. You can tell that important things are happening. Every interaction and every impression a child receives by seeing, tasting, touching, smelling, and hearing affects the development of the child's brain and builds new abilities. What and how children learn during the first 3 years become the building blocks for successful lifelong learning.

The relationships you build with children and the experiences you provide for them build the foundation for school success. From birth, young children begin developing language and literacy skills. They are communicators, eager to let you know what they need and think, and eager to engage you in interactions. Young children think mathematically, comparing who has more, putting things in order by size, noticing different shapes, matching, and sorting. They are also scientists, examining and manipulating everything that comes within their reach and trying to figure out how things work, how they grow, and what people do. They develop these abilities and understandings more readily when they have positive and trusting relationships with the important adults in their lives.

The third component of *The Creative Curriculum*® explains what infants, toddlers, and twos are learning. This chapter covers four main topics:

The Foundation for All Learning discusses the social–emotional characteristics and attitudes that influence the way children learn.

Building Language and Literacy Skills describes how children acquire skills to communicate, learn to hear and produce the sounds of language, engage with books and stories, and explore writing.

Discovering Mathematical Relationships discusses children's emerging understandings about number concepts, patterns, geometry and space. It also explains how children gain some understandings about the world by sorting and classifying.

Exploring Like Scientists describes what young children are learning about the physical world of objects, the natural world of animals and plants, and the social world of people.

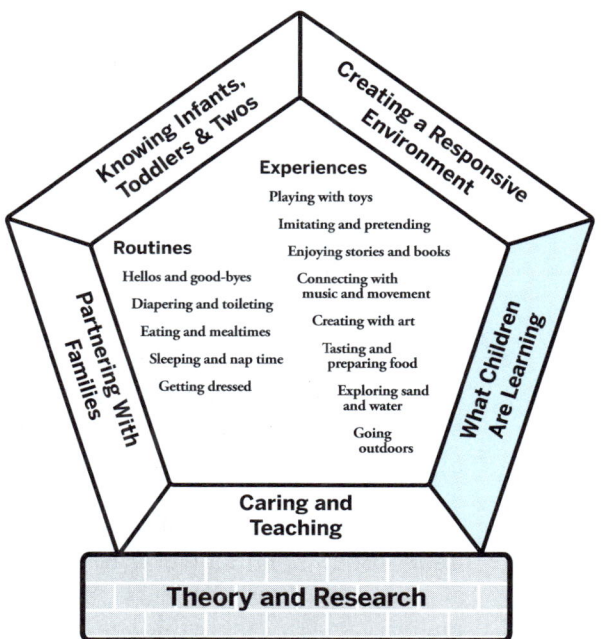

Chapter 3: **What Children Are Learning**

The Foundation for All Learning

School readiness is an important issue today. Children who enter school ready to learn have strong social–emotional skills and positive attitudes toward learning. How children feel about themselves and how they relate to others influence what and how they learn. School readiness actually begins in infancy.

For very young children, learning depends on the trusting relationships they build with the important adults in their lives. The research on relationships, especially the importance of secure attachments, explains how young children develop strong social and emotional skills when their needs are consistently met by trusted adults and when they have positive interactions with those adults. When they know that they are safe, loved, and cared for, children are ready to venture out to explore everything around them. When adults encourage these explorations and share children's excitement about new discoveries, children gain confidence in themselves as learners.

ZERO TO THREE: National Center for Infants, Toddlers, and Families identifies seven social–emotional characteristics that are essential for school-readiness. These traits are more fundamental to children's success than knowing letters and numbers.[18] They are listed here with definitions and examples of how children show these characteristics.

1. **Confidence:** a person's sense of control over his own behavior and environment; children's expectation that they will be able to succeed and adults will help them if necessary. Children with confidence are eager to try new things; show pleasure when they make a discovery or complete a task by clapping their hands, smiling, and looking at you; know their own names and use words like "my" and "me."

2. **Curiosity:** a desire to find things out, knowing the process will be enjoyable. Children demonstrate curiosity when they actively explore and investigate objects and materials using all of their senses; notice new things in the environment; ask questions about what, why, and how things happen, and try to figure out how things work.

3. **Intentionality:** the drive to make things happen and a determination to persist and not give up. Children show intentionality when they choose what they want to play with, take an interest in sounds and sights around them, stay with an activity for a period of time and complete it, and try different ways to solve a problem.

4. **Self-control:** children's ability to control their actions in age-appropriate ways. Children demonstrate self-control when they are receptive to redirection, increasingly behave in ways that are expected by adults, and learn to express and manage their feelings.

5. **Relatedness:** children's ability to engage with others, knowing they will be understood. Children who have acquired this characteristic trust familiar adults and have secure attachments, enjoy playing games such as peek-a-boo, take an interest in what other children are doing, are increasingly aware of the emotions of others, and enjoy playing with other children.

6. **Capacity to communicate:** the desire and ability to exchange ideas, feelings, and thoughts with others. Children communicate, first through crying, coos, gestures, and facial expressions, and eventually with words or signs. They are able to express ideas and feelings verbally or by signing, ask and answer questions, and converse.

7. **Cooperativeness:** the ability to engage with others in an activity or task, balancing their own needs with those of others to accomplish something. Children who are cooperative may imitate others and then join in, participate in small-group activities, begin to follow simple classroom rules, help put away toys or wipe a table, and offer to help another child.

Young children develop these characteristics when they are with adults who genuinely care about them, talk with them in calm and respectful ways, take joy in their discoveries, have appropriate expectations about what they can do, and guide their behavior in positive ways. Every interaction you have with a child is an opportunity to nurture these seven characteristics that are essential to children's success as learners. The next chapter, "Caring and Teaching," offers specific strategies for helping every child build a strong foundation for learning.

Building Language and Literacy Skills

A baby's brain is primed for acquiring language. When young children are around caring and responsive adults who talk with them, engage them in conversations, read to them every day, and teach them songs and rhymes, they are eager to communicate. Because infants, toddlers, and twos are very motivated to engage with others and communicate, you can make a difference that will last a lifetime.

Infants, toddlers, and twos need you to offer intentional experiences every day in order for them to acquire the building blocks of language and literacy. These include experiences that enable children to acquire vocabulary and language skills, hear the different sounds and rhythms of language, enjoy books and stories, and explore writing.

Vocabulary and Language

One of the greatest achievements in the first 3 years of life is the development of oral language. This includes the ability to understand the words that they hear (receptive language) and to put their own ideas and feelings into words so they can communicate with others (expressive language). A child with a good vocabulary and language skills can engage in conversations, share ideas and feelings, ask and answer questions, and work through problems.

Chapter 3: **What Children Are Learning**

From the time they utter their first word around their first birthday, until they are about 3 years old, children learn words and how to put them together at an astounding rate. Their language learning is supported by caring and responsive adults who talk to them, label and describe experiences and objects, and engage them in conversations.

People once thought it is not important to talk to babies because they do not understand what is being said. We now know that adults should use every opportunity from birth to talk to babies, describe things, reassure them, and sing to them.

Some children come from homes (and programs) where they hear 215,000 words every week (around 30,700 words a day). Compare that with children who hear only 62,000 words each week (around 8,800 words a day).[19] By age 3, the difference in the vocabularies and language use in these two groups of children is tremendous. Children who have rich language and literacy experiences usually have about twice the vocabulary of children who do not.

Researchers have found that language experiences in the first 3 years are one of the most reliable ways to predict reading ability by third grade.[20] Reading, after all, is getting meaning from the printed text. The more words a child knows, the more he understands when someone reads to him and, later, when he learns to read, himself. Once children fall behind, it is very hard for them to catch up. In school, they fall further and further behind. You can make sure that the infants, toddlers, and 2-year-olds in your care hear and learn to use a lot of language.

Children will show you in many ways that you are helping them develop vocabulary and language skills.[21]

A **young infant** might...

- calm down when you sing a favorite lullaby or talk to him in a quiet, reassuring voice
- turn her head toward you and smile when you speak to her
- make sounds directed to you, listen intently when you imitate the sounds, then repeat the sounds again and again
- lift his arms up when you come to his crib and ask, "Do you want to get up?"
- make sounds like "Ma-ma" and "Da-da"

A **mobile infant** might...

- understand some words: wave her hands when you say, "Bye-bye," or point to a ball when you ask, "Where's the ball?"
- string sounds together and repeat the sounds in a sing-song voice that begins to sound like speech: "Ba-ba-BA-BA-BA-ba-ba-ba"
- point toward and look at an object he wants, saying, "Uh, uh"; then look at you and back at the object, repeating the sound until you hand him what he wants
- respond when you ask, "Where is your nose?" by pointing to her nose
- use 10–50 single words that refer to people, objects, and events, simplifying some words (for example, *ba* for *bottle*, *ma* for *more*, *bow-wow* for *dog*)
- communicate with signs or pictures if he is unable to speak

A **toddler** might…

- point to different body parts as you sing a song like "Head and Shoulders, Knees and Toes"
- combine words into two-word sentences: "Daddy car." "More milk."
- use a questioning intonation to ask questions: "What dat?" or "Go out?" or "Where mommy?"
- answer simple questions: respond when you ask, "Where is your coat?" by showing you her coat
- understand and respond when you say, "Let's put the blocks in the box."
- learn 50–200 words by age 2
- use signs or pictures in a sequence to express an idea: *baby + cry*

- A **2-year-old** might…
- begin to use language to get information by asking *who, where, what,* and *why* questions: "Why you going?" "What this?" "Where teddy?"
- use language to express ideas and feelings: "No go outside."
- use 2- to 5-word sentences to communicate
- begin to use prepositions (*in, on*), pronouns (*me, he, we*), negatives (*can't, don't*), and conjunctions (*and*)
- understand and follow directions and simple stories

The Sounds and Rhythms of Language

The ability to hear and distinguish the sounds and rhythms of language is a very important skill for reading. During the preschool years, most children develop *phonological awareness,* the ability to hear the small units of sound in spoken language. They notice rhyming words in songs, poems, fingerplays, and stories. They enjoy playing with words, such as saying "Banana-fana-fo-fana." Preschoolers begin to hear and clap the syllables in their names: Son-ya; Ty-rone. They also notice that some words start with the same sound: *cat* and *cake*; *Denise* and *Danny*.

During the first 3 years of life, the brain is very receptive to learning the sounds that make up language. Every language has its own set of sounds that are used to form words. These sounds are called *phonemes*. If children are with adults who talk and sing with them, they pay attention to the sounds and rhythms of the languages they hear. By around 6 months of age, infants have learned to babble and repeat the sounds that make up the languages they hear.

Children under age 3 can develop *sound awareness,* the ability to notice and recognize different sounds, which is the first step in developing phonological awareness. Newborns have the ability to distinguish their mother's and father's voices from other voices or noises they hear around them. You may have noticed that young infants pay particular attention to the type of speech called *parentese*. When you talk slowly in a high pitched, sing-song voice, face-to-face with an infant, he is likely to pay attention to you long before he understands what you are saying. You may feel a bit silly, talking this way, but it is very effective in getting infants to listen to your voice.

Everyday experiences help children develop sound awareness. When you talk with children, play songs and sing the lyrics, recite nursery rhymes, and do fingerplays, you are helping children become aware of the sounds and rhythms of their language. When you make such experiences a part of your everyday work with young children, they will develop this very important awareness.

A **young infant** might…

- recognize his mother's or father's voice before he sees them
- put sounds together ("ba-ba-ba"), listen intently when you imitate them, then repeat the sounds again and again
- calm when she hears you sing the same lullaby she hears at home

A **mobile infant** might…

- string sounds together in a sing-song voice
- anticipate the part of a song where you do something interesting: "Trot, trot to Boston. Trot, trot to Lyn. Watch out, Jeremy! Don't fall…IN!"
- make the sounds of animals and things: "Baa-baa"; "Choo-choo"

A **toddler** might…

- repeat the refrain from a song she has heard many times: "E-I-E-I-O"
- fill in the rhyming word in a predictable refrain when you pause before saying the word
- recognize familiar sounds in the environment: the siren on a fire truck, a chirping bird, a car horn, the ring of a phone

A **2-year-old** might…

- play with the sounds in words you have taught her, for example "Nanabana"
- make up their own word games: "Silly, Willy, Billy"
- repeat words they enjoy hearing: "Pop, pop, pop"
- repeat familiar phrases from songs and rhymes

Enjoying Books and Stories

Reading books and sharing your pleasure in language and stories are among the most important gifts you can give to infants, toddlers, and twos. Children who regularly hear stories read aloud develop a foundation for literacy, including the motivation to learn to read. That is a key ingredient for success in school. Most children who enjoy being read to develop a love for books that will last throughout their lives, enriching their experiences and stretching their imaginations.

Long before infants can focus their eyes on the pictures, turn the pages, and understand the words you are saying, they can begin to associate books with the pleasant feelings they have when you hold them on your lap and share a book. Sharing books with infants, toddlers, and twos also builds other important literacy skills.

Vocabulary and language—Children learn new words as you share books about a variety of objects, actions, events, and places; link ideas in books with events and objects in children's lives; and repeat words from books during daily routines. Books for twos contain words that are less commonly heard, and they often include more complex sentences than the conversational language used with very young children in daily life. The descriptive language in books and the synonyms for familiar words help stretch children's language skills. Rich vocabularies and background knowledge are essential for children's later comprehension of school texts.

How print works—Toddlers and twos begin to learn about print when you point out words and letters, run you finger under print, and talk about what you are doing as you handle a book (for example, "Let's turn to the next page"). They begin to realize that pictures and print are meaningful and that books in English are read from front to back, one page at a time.

Letters and words—Some twos are beginning to recognize a few letters, usually the first letters of their names and some letters in environmental print, such as the *M* in the McDonald's logo or the *S* in a stop sign. They may enjoy finding these letters in simple alphabet books.

Comprehension—This is the ability to make sense of what is heard or read. Infants take their first steps toward comprehending print when they point to pictures in a book. Toddlers and twos begin to relate events in a story to their own lives, and older twos begin to retell familiar stories.

Understanding books and other texts—As you read stories to young children, they become aware that stories have beginnings and endings. They begin to understand that the phrase "Once upon a time" starts some stories and "The End" signals the end of some stories.

Phonological awareness—The types of books you read to children help them become aware of the sounds of language. Sound awareness, which is the first step in the development of phonological awareness, is discussed in the previous section.

As you share books and stories with young children, you will be rewarded by how much they are learning from these experiences.[22]

A **young infant** might…

- gaze at the bright pictures in a book you are holding or one that is propped up where she can see it
- wave, suck, chew, and manipulate the pages of a cardboard or cloth book
- vocalize as you read a book with simple, repetitive language

A **mobile infant** might…

- play with the moving parts of a book (for example, tabs to push, open, or pull)
- help you turn the pages of a book as you hold it and read
- hand you a book; then snuggle against you for as long as ten minutes as you read and talk about the pictures
- laugh or smile when he sees a familiar picture in a book you are sharing
- make sounds and point to pictures as you read each page
- point correctly to the picture of a familiar object when you ask where it is (for example, "Where's the dog?" "Can you show me the baby's eyes? Where are the baby's ears?")
- shake his head when you read a book like *Is Your Mama a Llama?* and you say, "No-o-o. My mama's a…"

A **toddler** might also…

- turn a book that is upside-down until it is rightside-up; then look at each page, turning one page at a time
- make animal noises or other appropriate sounds, such as "Moo, moo" or "Choo, choo," in response to pictures or something you read
- pretend to read the story, babbling as if she is reading the text
- point to a picture and ask, "What dat?"
- make connections between the content of a story and what he sees around him (for example, get a truck after seeing one in a book)
- fill in the next word when you pause before a rhyming word; repeat the words in a familiar predictable book

A **2-year-old** might also…

- select books on her own and pretend to read a familiar story, repeating phases accurately, especially from predictable books
- talk about the events or characters in a story: "Grandpa and me went to zoo. We saw tigers. And lions, too!"
- protest when you misread a familiar word or leave out a word
- ask to read you a favorite book again and again
- retell some of the details of a familiar story
- comment on the characters in a book (for example, "That cat'pillar is hungry.")

See chapter 13, "Enjoying Stories and Books," for ideas about selecting books and making reading experiences enjoyable for infants, toddlers, and twos.

Exploring Writing

Reading and writing go together. A group of letters is a symbol for a word, just as letters are symbols for sounds. Long before children can recognize letters and read or write letters and words, they begin to understand that one thing can represent something else. For example, a picture of a banana can represent a real banana; a block can stand for a car; particular golden arches mean McDonald's.

Children learn about writing if they see print in their environment, hear it read aloud, and see you writing for different reasons. Toddlers and twos are fascinated when they see you writing. They want to imitate what you do. At first, they have no idea what you are doing; they simply notice that you are taking an object, moving it across a piece of paper, and leaving marks. Over time and with experience, they begin to understand the purposes of writing.

Older infants, toddlers, and twos can begin to learn about and experiment with writing if they see pictures and print and if you give them drawing, painting, and writing tools.

A **mobile infant** might…

- watch as you write a note
- make random marks on paper with large crayons

A **toddler** might…

- grasp a large crayon and bang it on a piece of paper to make marks
- draw horizontal and some vertical lines, and circular marks
- move a paintbrush across a large sheet of paper until it is almost completely covered with paint
- make lines and circles in finger paint; then cover them up and repeat the process

A **2-year-old** might…

- experiment to see what kinds of marks she can make: lines, dots, zigzags
- make a series of looped scribbles and tell you, "This my mommy."
- tell you he wants to write a letter and then scribble all over a piece of paper
- point to her name on her cubby and tell you, "My name."
- begin to recognize common symbols in the environment and some letters, especially the first letter in his name
- draw lines and make marks that begin to look like letters
- ask you to write something for her, such as a story or letter that she dictated or her name on a picture

Promoting Language and Literacy Learning

Children gain language and literary skills when you offer them rich experiences and materials and talk with them. The chart that follows summarizes what you can do and say to promote their learning.

Language and Literacy Learning	What You Can Do and Say
Vocabulary and Language	• Explain what you are doing during routines: "I'm going to change your diaper now. You will feel much better when we're finished. First I'm going to…" • Use a high-pitched, sing-song voice and talk face-to-face with infants to get their attention. Speak slowly, and use short sentences and simple speech. • Converse by listening attentively and engaging in back-and-forth exchanges. Use gestures, facial expressions, or other cues to increase their understanding. • Describe what a child is doing: "You like those nesting cups, don't you? You like banging them together. Now you're banging them on the floor. Look! You put one inside the other, and it fit!" • Expand on what a child says: When he says, "Go out," you can say, "Do you want to go outside to play?" If she says, "More milk," you can say, "You finished all of your milk. You must have been thirsty. Now you want more milk. Here it is." • Share picture books with photos or objects that children can point to and name. • Ask open-ended questions to encourage children to verbalize their ideas. If a toddler points to her shoes and says, "New shoes," you can say, "I see that you have new shoes. They are blue. How did you get those shoes?" • Listen carefully and wait patiently as children express themselves. Do not rush them. • Label storage containers and shelves with picture and word labels. • Describe and talk about what children see, hear, feel, taste, and smell, for example, on a walk outdoors.

Language and Literacy Learning	What You Can Do and Say
Sounds and Rhythms of Language	• Imitate an infant's babbling and encourage her to imitate the sounds you make: "I hear you saying, 'Ma-ma-ma-ma.' Now you're saying it back to me." • Recite nursery rhymes, clapping along with the beat: "Patty cake, patty cake baker's man. Bake me a cake as fast as you can." • Talk about the sounds animals make: "What does a cow say? Moo. What does a dog sound like? Woof-woof." • Sing songs that encourage children to listen for and anticipate an action: "Ring around the rosie....Ashes, ashes, we all fall DOWN!" "Open, shut them....but DO NOT PUT THEM IN." • Sing, recite nursery rhymes, and do fingerplays with children, emphasizing the words that rhyme and words that start with the same sound. • Read stories with rhymes and lots of repetition, such as *Is Your Mama a Llama?*, *Good Night Moon*, and simple Dr. Seuss books. • Read stories with rhyming refrains and pause when you get to the rhyming word so children can fill it in: "Brown Bear, Brown Bear, what do you see? I see a red bird looking at ...." • Play with words: "See you later, alligator." "Let's comb your hair, you little bear." • Call attention to similarities of words: "*Tanya* and *Timmy* both start with the same sound: /t/. I'm going to tap, tap, tap, Timmy's toes, toes, toes. I'm going to tap, tap, tap, Tanya's nose, nose, nose."
Enjoying Stories and Books	• Provide cloth and soft plastic books that young infants can grasp, chew, and manipulate; cardboard books for mobile infants; and a range of story and content books for toddlers and twos. Display them attractively where children can reach them. • Hold infants on your lap as you read and show them books with simple, bright pictures. • Talk about the pictures. Label pictures a child points to: "That's a bottle, just like yours." Ask the child to find a picture, and ask questions about it: "Does he look happy?" • Let children play with and manipulate the book as you read, and encourage them to help you turn the pages. • Encourage children to chime in as you read a predictable book with repeated phrases. • Read books to children and tell stories every day, one-on-one and with small groups.

Language and Literacy Learning	What You Can Do and Say
Exploring Writing	• Let infants and toddlers see you writing and talk about what you are doing: "I'm making a list of what I need to buy so we can make pancakes tomorrow." • Point out print in the environment, such as letters on alphabet blocks, children's clothing, or displays. • Make picture and word labels for materials in the room, and label children's cubbies and belongings with their names. • Show and talk about pictures: "This is a picture of your mommy and daddy." "Can you find the picture of the puppy on this page?" • Provide large crayons, water-based markers, paint and brushes, and large chalk for toddlers and twos. Offer plenty of plain paper so they can use these tools to make marks, scribble, paint, and explore writing.

There are four objectives for literacy development and learning:

Objective 15. Demonstrates phonological awareness
a. Notices and discriminates rhyme
b. Notices and discriminates alliteration
c. Notices and discriminates smaller and smaller units of sound

Objective 16. Demonstrates knowledge of the alphabet
a. Identifies and names letters
b. Uses letter–sound knowledge

Objective 17. Demonstrates knowledge of print and its uses
a. Uses and appreciates books
b. Uses print concepts

Objective 18. Comprehends and responds to books and other texts
a. Interacts during read-alouds and book conversations
b. Uses emergent reading skills
c. Retells stories

Objective 19. Demonstrates emergent writing skills
a. Writes name
b. Writes to convey meaning

Discovering Mathematical Relationships

Mathematical thinking involves noticing similarities and differences; organizing information; and understanding quantity, numbers, patterns, space, and shapes. Learning the concepts and language of math—*more, less, smaller, the same as, how many*—gives children a sense of order and a way to make predictions and comparisons and to solve problems.

Infants, toddlers, and twos discover mathematical relationships every day when they explore space, compare amounts, and sort and match objects. As Jean Piaget and Lev Vygotsky explained, young children need many opportunities to explore and manipulate interesting objects in their environment and to be with adults who take an interest in what they are doing and talk to them about their discoveries.[23]

As you promote children's mathematical thinking, it helps to know what math concepts are important and what experiences are appropriate. The building blocks for understanding mathematics include experiences with number concepts, patterns and sequence, geometry and spatial relationships, and sorting and classifying.[24]

Number Concepts

Basic number concepts involve three different abilities: the ability to repeat a sequence of numbers in a particular order; to match each number with one of the items being counted; and to compare groups or quantities to determine relative amounts, that is, to know which has *more, less,* or the *same*.

Older infants, toddlers, and twos can begin to develop some understandings about number concepts when adults use numbers in everyday activities, sing songs that involve numbers, invite twos to help set the table for lunch, and provide materials they can explore in a variety of ways.

A **young infant** might…

- look at you intently as you put on her socks and say, "Here's one sock for this foot, and one sock for your other foot. Two feet, two socks."
- smile when you bring more cereal and ask, "Do you want *more* cereal? You must be hungry!"

A **mobile infant** might…

- place a lid on each container with which he is playing
- reach for more objects with which to play
- make a sign for "more" after finishing a cracker

A **toddler** might…

- stomp around the room, singing, "One, two, one, two, five."
- help you place one brush in each container of paint at the easel
- put a cup on each plate or a napkin next to each chair at the lunch table
- notice that another child has a larger lump of dough and ask you for more

A **2-year-old** might…

- line up a set of cars and place one block next to each car
- build a tower with blocks and announce, "Mine bigger."
- hold up two fingers when you ask, "How old are you?" and say, "I two."

Patterns and Relationships

Patterns are regular arrangements of objects, colors, shapes, numbers, or events. The ability to figure out a pattern involves recognizing the relationships that make up the pattern. It might be a pattern of sizes (large, small, large, small). It could be a pattern of colors (red, blue, red, blue) or a pattern of daily events ("After my cereal, I get a bottle.").

To begin to develop the ability to recognize patterns and relationships, young children first need many opportunities to explore and manipulate objects and notice similarities and differences.

A **young infant** might…

- focus on the color or texture of your dress
- wave her arms in anticipation when you arrive with her bottle
- stroke a rough carpet; feel the smooth tile floor

A **mobile infant** might…

- open his mouth when you lift a spoon toward his face
- play with nesting cups, trying different sizes until she finds one that fits inside another
- place several small blocks in a line, scatter them around the floor, and then collect and line them up again

A **toddler** might…

- beat a drum, imitating the way you are doing so
- use a small cup to fill a larger one with sand
- say a repetitive phrase from a story book while you read it aloud
- point to the Papa Bear in a book when you ask, "Which bear is bigger?"

A **2-year-old** might…

- line up cars of different sizes, grouping the big ones together and the little ones together
- group all the green pegs together and the red pegs together in a pegboard
- place rings on a graded stacking toy in order of size
- beat a drum after hearing you shake a tambourine

Geometry and Spatial Relationships

An understanding of geometry and spatial sense begins with the ability to recognize similar shapes and body positions in space. Children gain spatial sense as they become aware of themselves in relation to objects and structures around them. They learn about location and position (*on, off, under, below, in, out*) and about distance (*near, far, next to*).

By playing with objects of different shapes, young children learn that some objects are similar to other objects. When you describe what they see ("The orange looks like a ball"), you help infants, toddlers, and twos begin to develop an understanding of geometry. Opportunities to build and explore structures of various sizes enable toddlers and twos to develop understandings about spatial relationships.

A **young infant** might…

- place his hands around a bottle, feeling its shape
- experience being wrapped in a blanket
- run her hands back and forth along the edge of a table

A **mobile infant** might…

- crawl through a tunnel, enjoying the feeling of being enclosed in a space where she can see out both ends
- bang blocks against different slots in a shape-sorting box until they fall through
- drop a ball into a basket

A **toddler** might…

- try to put a teddy bear into a box that is too small; then find a larger box and put the bear into it
- handle 3-dimensional shapes and put all the cubes in a bucket
- know whether to go *around, in,* or *through* a structure in order to get to an object

A **2-year-old** might…

- blow bubbles outdoors and say, "Look! Balls. Lot of balls."
- learn the names of some shapes: "This a circle. It's like a pizza."
- bend down to look when you say, "Your shoes are under the table."

Sorting and Classifying

Every day, we think mathematically when we organize information in a logical way in order to make comparisons. Preschoolers, for example, might make a collection of leaves, sort them into piles according to type, and then compare how many they have of each type. Sorting and classifying involves the ability to notice similarities and differences. It also involves the ability to organize a collection of objects according to one attribute, such as size, color, shape, or function.

Infants, toddlers, and twos become familiar with similarities and differences by using all of their senses as they explore. They learn by watching, listening, touching, smelling, and tasting. By manipulating objects, they learn how objects are the same and different. When you describe what they are discovering, you help them become aware of different characteristics.

A **young infant** might…

- recognize your voice when he hears you say, "I'm coming. I hear you calling me."
- distinguish between familiar and unfamiliar adults
- show a preference for a particular soft blanket and enjoy stroking it

A **mobile infant** might…

- hit a xylophone with a wooden stick but shake a rattle
- pick out all the oranges pieces from a fruit salad
- collect wooden blocks and put them in a box

A **toddler** might…

- see a picture of a donkey and say, "Horsie."
- place a blue block next to another blue block
- place differently shaped blocks into the matching openings in the shape-sorter box

A **2-year-old** might…

- put all of the yellow blocks in a bucket
- pick out all of the round beads from a pile of assorted beads
- select all of the cubic blocks from a pile of different shapes and then build a tower

Helping Children Discover Mathematical Relationships

The experiences and materials you provide for infants, toddlers, and twos can help them begin to discover mathematical relationships. The next chart lists important mathematical concepts and skills and shows what you can do to encourage children's mathematical thinking.

Discovering Mathematical Relationships	What You Can Do and Say
Number Concepts: Counting	• Recite nursery rhymes that include numbers, such as "One, Two, Buckle My Shoe." • Sing songs and fingerplays that use numbers, for example, "1-2-3-4-5, I caught a fish alive," and "Three little ducks that I once knew…" • Read stories that include numbers. • Count with children: "Let's see how many trucks we have. One, two, three. We have three trucks."
Number Concepts: Noticing Relative Sizes and Amounts	• Provide toys that engage infants and toddlers in exploring different sizes, such as nesting cups and stacking rings. • Use comparison words: "You picked out the *biggest* ball." "You're telling me that you want *more* peaches." • Put containers of various sizes in the sand and water tubs.
Patterns and Relationships (Recognizing repeated units)	• Sings repetitive songs. • Read predictable books with a repeated language pattern, for example, *Brown Bear, Brown Bear, What Do You See?*. • Point out patterns so children become aware of them. "Look at the stripes on your shirt: a red stripe, and then a yellow one. Red, and then yellow again." "You lined up the cars: a big car; then a little one; then a big one, and then a little one." • Provide toys that children can use to make patterns, such as colored wooden blocks, large beads and laces, large peg boards and pegs.

Discovering Mathematical Relationships	What You Can Do and Say
Geometry and Spatial Relationships (Recognizing shapes and positions in space)	• Provide large cardboard boxes and tunnels so children can crawl in and out, and over and under, and experience different positions in space: *inside, outside, over, under*. • Talk about 2- and 3-dimensional shapes and link them to common objects: "That block is shaped like a train car." • Use positional words: "Let's put all the balls *in* the box." "Keisha is sitting *next to* Tyrone." • Include materials that children can use to build structures, such as Duplos® and blocks.
Sorting and Classifying (Matching by one characteristic)	• Organize toys on the shelves and in containers labeled with pictures and words. • Point out groups that children have made: "You put all the red pegs in a row." "You seem to like the blue cars best." • Provide older toddlers and twos with collections that they can organize in different ways, such as large plastic bottle caps, plastic animals, pinecones, and shells.

There are four objectives for mathematics development and learning:

Objective 20. Uses number concepts and operations
a. Counts
b. Quantifies
c. Connects numerals with their quantities

Objective 21. Explores and describes spatial relationships and shapes
a. Understands spatial relationships
b. Understands shapes

Objective 22. Compares and measures

Objective 23. Demonstrates knowledge of patterns

Exploring Like Scientists

Science involves finding answers to interesting questions. What does this feel like? How does this work? Why did this happen? What would happen if we tried it another way? How can we make this work better?

Scientists are curious and eager investigators. They wonder about what they see, try their ideas, observe what happens, and draw conclusions. A new discovery often leads them to investigate more. Opportunities to explore and investigate are everywhere.

Young children are born scientists. They are curious about everything. Infants investigate their surroundings by using all of their senses. They spend a lot of time gazing at things, but, once they are mobile, they are off on their own to find out how things also feel, taste, smell, and sound. Toddlers and twos experiment, trying to discover to how things work, what things do, and what they can make happen. They are fascinated by animals and people and what makes plants grow. Like scientists, young children are curious about and want to investigate the physical, natural, and social worlds around them.

The Physical World

Physical science involves exploring the physical properties of objects and materials. Children gather information about the physical world by using all of their senses to explore and investigate. What does this feel like? Slimy, squishy, hard, or sticky? How does this smell? Is it loud or quiet? Is it fast or slow? How can I make this move? Can I roll it, twist it, blow on it, or push it? What will happen if I drop this on the floor?

Throughout the day, you will see young children touching, tasting, looking at, listening to, smelling, and manipulating objects to learn about the physical world around them.

A **young infant** might…

- grasp and mouth a teething ring you offer
- mouth and then shake a rattle you place in her hand
- bat at a hanging toy to make it move (testing cause and effect)
- pull a string attached to a toy to make it come closer
- raise his bottle when the milk level drops and continue sucking

A **mobile infant** might…

- pull aside a blanket after watching you hide a toy because she expects it to exist even when she cannot see it (object permanence)
- repeatedly drop objects on the floor to see what happens
- push the buttons on a pop-up toy to make different things appear; then push them down and start over again
- watch you make a soft toy squeak; then squeeze it to reproduce the sound
- open drawers and cabinets to investigate what is inside; then take everything out

A **toddler** might…

- push a chair across the room and stand on it to reach a toy
- experiment to see what sounds he can make on a xylophone and with musical bells
- pick up acorns in the play yard, drop them on the slide, and watch them roll down and across the ground; then run to collect them and repeat the whole process again and again

A **2-year-old** might…

- try using different tools at the water table: watering cans, cups of different sizes, funnels, scoops, sponges, and basters
- use a plastic screwdriver and hammer on a toy workbench to turn bolts and pound pegs
- mix paint colors to make new colors
- use words to describe the properties of objects: *hard, smooth, heavy, sticky*

The Natural World

Life science involves exploring the natural world of living things, including both plants and animals. What does the rabbit like to eat? How loud can I make my voice? What will happen if I pick this flower? Where did all these leaves come from?

A **young infant** might…

- discover her toes, grab her feet, and try to put them into her mouth
- touch your mouth as you sing, to investigate where the sound is coming from
- play with your hair as you hold him
- observe a fish in a bowl with interest

A **mobile infant** might…

- look into a tree when she hears birds chirping
- play with the grass and dandelions in the play yard
- enjoy the sound of crunching leaves as he crawls on the playground
- reach to pet a friendly dog

A **toddler** might…

- get excited when he sees a squirrel scamper across the yard and up a tree
- collect leaves and play with them inside
- pretend that a doll is a baby and take her for a walk in a stroller
- fill a pail with damp sand, pat it down, and turn it upside down to make a cake

A **2-year-old** might…

- watch a line of marching ants and try to figure out where they are going
- ask you, "Where snow go?" after observing that the snowman she helped build the day before had melted
- help you water the plants in the outdoor garden and understand that water helps plants grow
- hold a carrot for the class rabbit to eat and say, "He hungry."

The Social World

Infants are more fascinated by people than anything else. They learn very quickly to distinguish familiar people from strangers. Before long, they can identify the people in their families and people who belong to other families. They are curious about who people are, what they do, and where they live.

Daily living teaches infants, toddlers, and twos about their social world.

A **young infant** might…

- get excited when she sees familiar people enter the room
- gaze at photographs of family members you have mounted on the wall
- watch other babies with great interest

A **mobile infant** might…

- play alongside another child, sometimes imitating what she is doing
- point to himself in the mirror when you ask, "Where is the baby?"
- stop playing to watch an unfamiliar person who entered the room

A **toddler** might…

- recognize that the face she sees in the mirror is her own
- join a group as you read a story
- act out simple life scenes, such as going to the doctor, talking on a phone, or feeding a baby
- offer a toy to another child

A **2-year-old** might…

- understand the sequence of routines (for example, remember where things are stored, get his special blanket when you say it is nap time, or go to wash hands when you announce that lunch is ready)
- pretend to be a firefighter when playing with a fire truck
- show an understanding of the rules (for example, say "No!" when another child tries to take something from her)
- identify himself as a boy
- show a great deal of interest in young babies and what they can and cannot do

Encouraging Children to Explore Like Scientists

To encourage infants, toddlers, and twos to explore like scientists as they engage with the physical, natural, and social worlds, the most important thing is to provide interesting things for them to observe, manipulate, and explore. Watch, appreciate, and talk to them about what they are doing and learning. Your interest and enthusiasm reinforces their desire to find out more and gives them confidence to continue to explore and experiment as scientists do.

Scientific Explorations	What You Can Do and Say
The Physical World	• Place objects in infants' hands that they can hold, manipulate, and mouth safely. • Give a baby a spoon to hold while you feed her with another spoon, explaining, "You can hold a spoon, too. Soon you will feed yourself." • Offer a basket with colorful fabric scraps of different textures for children to examine. • Provide collections of objects for children to explore and play with, such as large plastic bottle caps, plastic containers, and balls. • Show interest in children's discoveries: "That dough feels soft and squishy, doesn't it?" "You figured out how to make music with those bells. You just shake, shake, shake them."
The Natural World	• Take children outdoors each day to experience plants and animals, the weather, and an entirely different environment. Point out what is happening: "I see that you are watching the clouds move in the sky." "What did you find? Those are acorns. Do you want to put them in a bucket?" • Provide natural materials for toddlers and twos to explore and examine: shells, pinecones, feathers. • Plant a small garden outdoors or have indoor plants that toddlers and twos can help care for. • Have a fish tank with a covered top and place it where children can watch the fish. For older toddlers and twos, have a class pet like a rabbit or guinea pig that they can help care for.
The Social World	• Assign a primary caregiver to each child so children develop secure attachments and learn to trust adults. • Keep group sizes small and help children learn to relate positively to others. • Talk about the different jobs of people in the program: cooks, drivers, teachers, the director. • Read stories about people and what they do. • Provide simple dress-up clothes, dolls, cars and trucks, and people figures. Engage children in imitating and pretending to do what other people do.

There are five objectives for science and technology development and learning, and five objectives for social studies:

Objective 24. Uses scientific inquiry skills

Objective 25. Demonstrates knowledge of the characteristics of living things

Objective 26. Demonstrates knowledge of the physical properties of objects and materials

Objective 27. Demonstrates knowledge of Earth's environment

Objective 28. Uses tools and other technology to perform tasks

Objective 29. Demonstrates knowledge about self

Objective 30. Shows basic understanding of people and how they live

Objective 31. Explores change related to familiar people or places

Objective 32. Demonstrates simple geographic knowledge

Conclusion

This chapter explained how the experiences you provide for infants, toddlers, and twos support learning in language and literacy, math, and science and prepare children for success in school and in life. You will find many more suggestions for selecting materials and nurturing children's learning and development in chapters 6–18, which discuss routines and experiences. Positive relationships and social–emotional skills were described as the base from which infants, toddlers, and twos acquire cognitive and language skills and knowledge about the world around them. The next chapter, "Caring and Teaching," addresses this important topic.

Caring and Teaching

Building Relationships — 106
Strategies for Building Trusting Relationships — 106
Helping Children Get Along With Others — 108
A Structure That Supports Relationships — 110
Helping Children Transition to a New Group or Preschool — 112

Promoting Children's Self-Regulation — 113
Setting the Foundation for Young Infants' Self-Regulation — 113
Helping Mobile Infants Begin to Control Their Behavior — 114
Promoting the Self-Regulation of Toddlers and Twos — 114
Using Positive Guidance Strategies — 116

Responding to Challenging Behaviors — 119
Physical Aggression — 119
Temper Tantrums — 120
Biting — 121

Guiding Children's Learning — 124
Learning Through Play — 125
Talking With Infants, Toddlers, and Twos — 127
Extending Children's Knowledge and Skills — 128
Including All Children — 129

Assessing Children's Development and Learning — 132
Step 1: Observing and Collecting Facts — 132
Step 2: Analyzing and Responding — 136
Step 3: Evaluating Each Child's Progress — 137
Step 4: Summarizing, Planning, and Communicating — 138

Caring and Teaching

Teaching and caring for infants and toddlers is interesting, fun, joyful, rewarding, and sometimes challenging and exhausting. You soothe a crying baby by snuggling in a glider, watch a mobile infant's first tentative steps with fascination, and laugh as she dumps big beads on the floor again and again. You gather a small group of toddlers to listen to a story, and sing and dance in front of the most nonjudgmental audience you will ever have. Children change so much during the first 3 years of life!

This chapter describes the fourth component of *The Creative Curriculum® for Infants, Toddlers & Twos* and examines the many different aspects of your role.

Building Relationships explains how to use your knowledge of child development and individual children's strengths and needs to build trusting, responsive relationships with and among children. Program policies and structure can help facilitate your efforts to build relationships.

Promoting Children's Self-Regulation suggests ways to help young children express their feelings and regulate their behavior in acceptable and appropriate ways. The section describes positive guidance strategies, including ways to organize the environment and adjust daily routines.

Responding to Challenging Behaviors offers strategies to manage children's inevitable challenging behaviors. Physical aggression, temper tantrums, and biting are discussed.

Guiding Children's Learning explains why everyday routines and experiences are important parts of your work. You help children learn as they play by paying attention to the ways you talk with them and encourage them to try new skills. This section also provides information and strategies for guiding the learning of children who are dual language learners and children with disabilities.

Assessing Children's Development and Learning describes how assessment is an ongoing process in which information is collected in order to make decisions. You use what you learn about each child to build responsive relationships; determine each child's strengths, needs, and interests; promote learning; and communicate with family members.

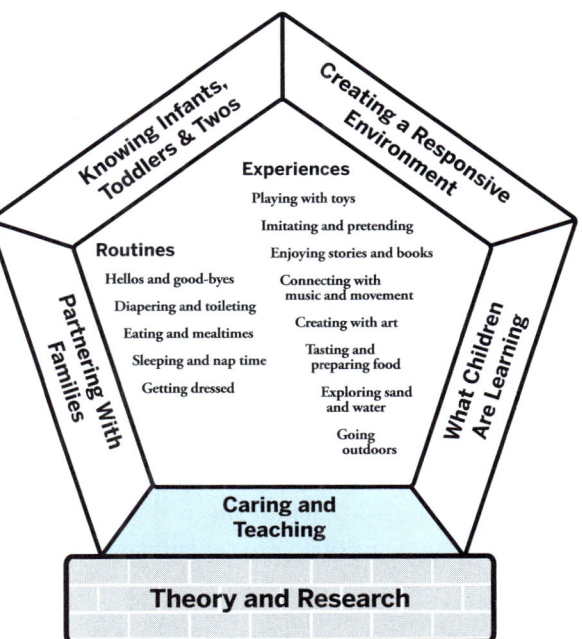

Building Relationships

Young children's development flourishes when they have close, supportive, and trusting relationships with the adults in their lives. Such relationships between children and teachers are the core of quality care. Knowing that you will meet their physical and social–emotional needs, children are able to explore and get to know the other people and objects in their environment. Your relationship fuels children's curiosity and desire to learn. Their connection with you allows them to feel safe enough to move, to explore, to experiment and, thereby, to learn.

Strategies for Building Trusting Relationships

Every interaction you have with children is an opportunity to build relationships that help them thrive. Here are some strategies to try.

Delight in the children who are in your care. Greet them affectionately each day. Show that you enjoy them. Laugh with them as they take their first halting steps, fall, and get up again. Smile at the toddler's emerging sense of humor. Celebrate each new accomplishment as you watch a child learn to roll over, sit up, walk, run, and jump. Delight as they coo and babble, speak their first words, and string words together to form sentences. Enjoy the closeness of holding a young infant in your arms and the special time you have reading a favorite story to a 2-year-old.

Relate in ways that build trust. Be dependable. Let children know that they can count on you. Be at the door to greet them each morning. Respond promptly to a child who is crying. Tell children when you are going to leave the room. Keep your promises: "Yesterday I said you could help make playdough today. Are you ready?" Remember that building relationships is a central part of your work. Slow down and spend time with children individually, every day.

Use caring words to let children know that they are respected, understood, and valued. Think about what you say and how you say it. Even infants who cannot yet talk and who do not know the meaning of your words are sensitive to the tone and volume of your voice. Use the child's home language whenever possible. Practice using caring words and a caring tone. For example, when comforting an upset child, you might say, "You are having a hard time. I can tell by your tears that you're feeling sad. Let's sit in the rocking chair together and figure out how to help you feel better."

Build relationships with all children, including those with whom you have more difficulty building positive relationships. As a professional, you need to figure out why you do not bond with some children as easily as with others. Perhaps you and the child have very different temperaments and personalities. As a first step, look for and focus on the positive characteristics of each child. Share your feelings with a colleague if you think this might help, or even ask a colleague to observe you and a child together.

Adapt daily routines to meet individual needs. Offer an infant a bottle when she is hungry, regardless of whether it is time for a scheduled snack or meal. Give a toddler time to finish his puzzle before you change his diaper. Handle children's bodies respectfully, even if it means that a routine will take longer. Explain to an infant, "I'm going to pick you up now so I can change your diaper." Ask a toddler, "Will you please help me take off your wet shirt?" Make daily routines into learning times.

Offer children opportunities to make decisions, whenever possible. Give children clear alternatives when a choice is theirs to make. For example, at snack time, ask children to choose among slices of banana, peach, or pear. This shows that you respect their tastes and their developing decision-making skills. You can even talk with young infants about choices: "Do you want to be rocked or rubbed? Let's see."

Be careful not to overstimulate children. Watch for signs that children are becoming overwhelmed, such as when an infant turns his head away during a conversation or a toddler is not able to sustain attention the way he usually does. Respond by changing your behavior or adjusting the environment so that the child can become calm and engaged.

Observe children closely to help you decide how best to respond. Give a child your full attention. Observe the child's facial expressions and body language. Learn to distinguish an infant's cries, so you will know whether the child is hungry or needs comforting. Learn how to calm an upset toddler. Use *Objectives for Development & Learning* to help you get to know and appreciate individual children and to decide how to respond to each child. Be aware of each child's personal style and how it might be culturally based. Respect each child's style of interaction. Some children jump into activities immediately and enthusiastically. Others need time to watch and may need some gentle encouragement.

Know yourself. Self-awareness requires a willingness to ask questions such as, "Why am I acting this way?" For example, you would want to identify why you are becoming overly involved with one child or shying away from another. Recognize that your feelings shape your interactions. Being aware of your feelings will help you form relationships and respond to children individually. Take a few minutes each day to take care of yourself so that you will have the focus and energy you need to give the children your full attention.

Helping Children Get Along With Others

The trusting relationships you build with each child help form the foundation for other relationships. When you treat children in loving, respectful, and consistent ways, you promote their positive attitudes toward others. Nevertheless, life in group care can be stressful for children. Interacting with individual children and with very small groups of children will give you and the children a break from the intensity of a larger group. One-on-one and small-group interactions also allow you to give each child more attention and to make more intimate connections than are possible in a large group.

Limit group activities for infants and always be flexible to respond to individual needs. Although they still need you to respond to their individual needs, toddlers in groups may begin to follow the same schedule for meals and naps. Toddlers and twos tend to group and regroup themselves throughout the day as they play at the water table, enjoy a painting experience that you organize, play in the rocking boat, or listen to a story. Twos often enjoy the addition of a very short morning greeting time.

Here are some strategies for helping children get along with others and manage life in a group setting.

Remember that children look to you as a model. The infants, toddlers, and twos you care for are very aware of what you do. The way you interact with each child, with colleagues, and with families teaches children more powerfully than anything you might say directly about how to get along with other people.

Arrange your environment so that children have opportunities to be in small groups when they want. Time away from the whole group offers a chance for social interactions that might not take place when everyone is together. Physical spaces that give children a break from group life and promote one-on-one interactions include a large cardboard box or a comfortable chair with room for two persons. You and one or two children can enjoy being together as you play peek-a-boo or prepare a snack.

Mirror the behavior of infants and toddlers. When you smile at an infant who is smiling at you or imitate the funny expression on a toddler's face, you acknowledge his experience and confirm that relating to others is worthwhile.

Acknowledge children's positive interactions. Comment when you see children engaging positively with each other. For example, when two 8-month-olds are sitting on a blanket together, you might say, "You are getting to know each other. You touched her face very gently."

> **Matthew** (22 months) is drawing a picture for his new sister. Mercedes comments, "You are drawing a picture for your sister. You must be thinking about her."

Give children opportunities to help you. Children begin to understand how to contribute positively to group life when you invite them to help you.

> **Barbara** asks Leo (18 months) and other children to carry a letter to the mailbox. She also asks them to help set out their mats at nap time. She encourages their understanding that these are ways to help other people.

Encourage children to help one another. Throughout the day, offer children opportunities to assist each other. For example, you might have occasions to invite one child to help look for another's missing sock. Acknowledge when a child uses words or gentle acts to comfort another child.

Read books about helpfulness and friendship. There are wonderful books for toddlers and twos, such as *The Enormous Turnip* and *Bear's Busy Family*. Children also love homemade books about familiar events and people they know, such as *Valisha Helps Jonisha Find Her Sweater*.

Offer interesting materials and experiences throughout the room. Purposeful room arrangement and thoughtful displays of toys and materials will help avoid the inevitable pushing and shoving that happens when too many toddlers are together in a small space.

Include equipment and materials that promote interaction and cooperation. Provide a wooden rocking boat that two or more children can rock together, offer large sheets of butcher paper for children to color or paint on together, and provide opportunities for group water and sand play.

Arrange the environment to help children begin to experience turn-taking and sharing. Placing three chairs around a small table helps children figure out whether there is a place for them or whether they have to come back when fewer children want to sit there. Providing duplicates of toys minimizes conflict over sharing, which is an unreasonable expectation for most toddlers and twos.

Allow children time to work out their differences, but be ready to step in if you are needed. For example, when you wait a few minutes before stepping in, you give two toddlers a chance to discover that there is room for both of them to sit on the sofa together. Watch closely so you can intervene if you see that one is about to be pushed off!

A Structure That Supports Relationships

Program policies and procedures can promote the ability of staff members to develop trusting, responsive relationships with children. Three factors help support relationship building.

Group sizes and teacher–child ratios are key to implementing high-quality programs. Small groups allow teachers to interact with children individually, take the time needed for daily routines, observe and respond to each child, and follow the child's lead. Group care can feel chaotic and overwhelming to very young children. Small group sizes help them feel safe and more secure.

The National Association for the Education of Young Children (NAEYC) recommends limiting group size to no more than eight infants ages birth–15 months. If there are six infants in the group, there should be at least one teacher for every three children. If there are eight infants in the group, there should be at least one teacher for every four children.

NAEYC also recommends limiting group size to no more than 12 children ages 12–36 months. For children ages 12–18 months, there should be 1 teacher for every 3 children when there are 6 children in the group and 1 teacher for every 4 children when there are 8–12 children in the group. For children ages 21–36 months, there should be 1 teacher for every 4 children when there are 8 children in the group, 1 teacher for every 5 children when there are 10 children in the group, and 1 teacher for every 6 children when there are 12 children in the group. The term *teacher* includes teachers, assistant teachers, and teacher aides.[25]

When a **primary caregiver** is assigned to each child, children and families benefit. This person has the major responsibility for a child's care and education, although other teachers participate as well. He or she is often the family's primary contact with the program.

By providing regular and consistent care, a primary caregiver becomes a child's secure base in child care. Children learn that they can trust this person to comfort them when they are tired, upset, or frightened and to help them as necessary as they explore and learn. Their relationship with a primary teacher helps children feel secure enough to relate to other adults.

Continuity of care refers to a program philosophy that supports children's staying with the same teacher for all—or at least most—of their first 3 years. Children under age 3 need continuity of care to feel safe and secure. It takes time for a child and teacher to form a secure attachment. They are less likely to form secure attachments when children change teachers frequently. Despite this knowledge, program policies often require that infants and toddlers move to new groups and new teachers when they reach a certain age or begin to walk. This transition is often very difficult for the child, as well as for teachers and families.

Here are some ways that programs can promote continuity of care:

- Children of the same age and teachers stay together in the same space until the children are 3 years old.
- Children are cared for in mixed age-groups and remain with the same teachers and children until they are ready for preschool.
- Children and teachers move together to a new space as children grow older.
- Groups divide. Some children from one group move with one teacher to another room, where they join a new teacher and a few children from her original group.
- Children remain with the same teacher until they are 18 months or 2 years old. They then move to a toddler or twos group.
- Children change teachers but visit their previous teachers whenever they wish.

Helping Children Transition to a New Group or Preschool

While infants, toddlers, and twos make many transitions throughout the day, major transitions occur when children move to a new group within your program and when they move to a new program, perhaps to go to preschool. By making these major transitions as smooth as possible for children and families, you help children build on their successes in your setting as they move to a new one. Change is harder for some children than for others, but some additional support is helpful for everyone. Children, families, and teachers may all feel sad about leaving the strong relationship you have built together over time. Introducing a child and family to new arrangements before the actual change gives them the opportunity to experience the new situation from the base of trust and security they have established with you.

Separation can evoke children's deep feelings. You may find that, during the last weeks or days before the change, a child becomes restless or more easily upset, tests limits more than usual, or may even get angry or frustrated with you. A child may cling to you or want to spend all of his time by your side. Even challenging behaviors show how much the child cares for you. Here are some ideas for making transitions easier for children, families, and you.

Think about transitions ahead of time. Develop program-wide plans for handling internal transitions. When possible, forge relationships with external preschool programs. Share information with a child's new program about your center and about *The Creative Curriculum*®. Lay the groundwork for a new teacher to get to know a child by sharing information and the insights you gained from ongoing assessment of the child's progress. Be sure that your program's director and the child's family approves of taking this step.

Talk with the family about how their child handles change and about strategies that help their child cope with change.

Plan to have the child and family visit the new group or program. Encourage them to visit more than once if possible. Invite the new teacher to visit the child in your setting so she can observe the child in a familiar place. If a child is changing teachers and rooms within a center, it is easy to make numerous visits. During these visits, take photos of the child in the new setting and with the new teacher. Make a book with photos from the new and old settings.

Talk about the change, beginning about 2 weeks before the transition. Take care not to convey your sorrow or concerns or to make too much of a planned change. Integrate your mention of the new setting or new teacher into your everyday interactions.

Celebrate the child's last day with a special snack or by singing a song you made up about the child. This gives you an opportunity to acknowledge the change through a small, low-key ritual. Be sure to say good-bye. Your acknowledgment is a sign of respect to the child, family, and the relationship you have worked so hard to build during the time you spent together.

Promoting Children's Self-Regulation

Developing self-regulation, the ability to control one's own feelings and behavior, is a primary task of early childhood. It takes time. Infants, toddlers, and twos have immediate and intense feelings of joy and excitement, as well as feelings of anger and frustration. They do not yet have the ability to stop and think about how to express their feelings in acceptable ways. They may not have the verbal language to express their feelings. Learning to self-regulate is a slow process that requires your patience and understanding of what each child is able to do at given stages of development.

Setting the Foundation for Young Infants' Self-Regulation

Self-regulation begins when you and a child's family gently establish patterns for routines and respond to the child in respectful, caring ways. You help an infant begin to learn to manage her feelings and behavior when, for example, you pick her up to comfort her or encourage her to sleep by following the same ritual. Here are some suggestions for setting the foundation for self-regulation as you care for young infants.

Establish and follow rituals, providing as much continuity with a child's home as possible. Singing the same songs or rocking a tired baby before laying her down helps her begin to learn how to organize her own behavior.

Use your face, voice, touch, and motion to help a young infant manage his feelings and other responses to stimulation. Holding a young infant, looking in her eyes, and talking to her quietly may help her calm herself and focus briefly on something that catches her interest. Observe and take steps throughout the day to ensure that children are not overwhelmed by the noise and confusion of group life.

Stay nearby when babies are lying or sitting close to each other. Be sure that everything within their reach is safe for children to play with and mouth.

Helping Mobile Infants Begin to Control Their Behavior

Mobile infants are movers who want to explore everything. While you do not want to discourage their eagerness to investigate and try their ideas, you do want to keep them safe. The goal is to set limits that they can understand and to set them in ways that show respect and help children be competent. Here are some suggestions.

Use simple, clear language to communicate which behaviors are acceptable. Let your facial expression and tone of voice emphasize your message: "You may use the crayons on the paper."

Use the word *no* sparingly. Save this for dangerous situations so it will be effective.

Give children many opportunities to move and be active throughout the day. Children who are happily engaged are less likely to get into dangerous situations and conflicts. Practice also helps children master new skills.

Plan the day so there are no long waits between routines and experiences. If children have to wait for a few minutes, then sing, do a fingerplay, or tell a story to help pass the time in an interesting, relaxed way.

Think about the situation from the children's perspective before intervening. For example, be aware that what looks like one child's grabbing a toy from another child may be a "taking away and giving back" game.

Give children the chance to work things out themselves if no one will be hurt. For example, a child may briefly react and then decide she does not care when someone picks up a toy with which she had been playing. In such a situation, your involvement would create unnecessary tension.

Promoting the Self-Regulation of Toddlers and Twos

The behavior of toddlers and twos can sometimes stretch your patience. It is also exciting to watch confident toddlers take the initiative to learn about themselves and their world by testing limits. Try to retain your sense of humor, keeping in mind that testing limits is developmentally appropriate behavior for children this age.

Here are some suggestions for promoting the self-regulation of toddlers and twos in positive ways so they are competent to learn rules and how to follow them.

Encourage their growing sense of independence. Invite them to participate in daily routines. Give them many chances to make choices. Organize the environment so children can hang up their coats and reach the sink to wash their hands.

Understand that toddlers and most twos are not yet ready to share. This does not mean that they are greedy or mean. They need time to develop a sense of ownership and learn first to take turns and then to share. Model and encourage taking turns and sharing, but do not insist on it. To help avoid conflicts, provide duplicates of favorite toys.

Share your feelings about particular behaviors. "I know that you are angry, and that's okay. I don't want people to hurt each other, though. I'm going to help you so you don't hit."

Give children alternative ways to express their anger. "If you feel angry, tell us. Say, 'I'm mad!' so we will know how to help you."

Ask toddlers silly questions so they have lots of opportunities to say *no*.

> **Matthew** (22 months) loves when Mercedes asks questions such as, "Do we eat a shoe for dinner?" or "Is it time to go to sleep after breakfast?"

Pay close attention to a child who is likely to hit or bite. Help the child stop the behavior before another child gets hurt.

Acknowledge children's actions when they show some self-control.

> **Barbara** saw Leo (18 months)—who was about to throw a block—catch her eye. He then put the block on the floor. "That was a good idea, Leo. You put the block down. You did not throw it."

Use familiar signals to let children know when it is time to move from one activity to another. For example, give a 2-minute warning when it is time to clean up. Dim the lights and play soft music when it is time for a nap. When children have a sense of what to expect, they tend to feel more secure and calm during transitions. With less confusion, challenging behaviors are less likely.

Avoid talking with other adults about a challenging behavior in front of the child whose behavior is a problem. Toddlers and twos are very aware of when they are the topic of conversation. Being talked about can be uncomfortable.

Toddlers and twos can begin to understand and follow a few simple, clear rules. Rules such as, "Sit at the table when you cut with scissors" give children a sense of order and security as well as the opportunity to develop self-regulation. Over time and after many reminders, children will learn to take their scissors to the table.

Think about what rules are absolutely essential. Rules should be as concrete as possible, few in number (no more than three or four), simple, and stated in positive terms. Rules generally fall into three categories:

- maintaining physical safety *(We care about each other.)*
- not hurting others *(We treat each other gently.)*
- caring for the room *(We use materials carefully.)*

Using Positive Guidance Strategies

Positive guidance can take many forms. For example, you arrange your environment to prevent dangerous or unacceptable behavior before it occurs. You prevent *dangerous behavior* when you cover an outlet or remove materials and equipment that are too difficult to use. You prevent *unacceptable behavior* when you adjust your daily routines to minimize noise, confusion, waiting, and large-group activities and to increase the time children can run and play outdoors. Here are some strategies for guiding children's behavior in positive ways as you help infants, toddlers, and twos learn to manage their feelings and behavior.

Give the big rule and the little rule. The big rule/little rule strategy for rules and limits involves stating one of your three or four main rules (the big rule) and pairing it with the very specific behavior in which you want the child to engage (the little rule).

> **Brooks** says to Abby (14 months), "Be safe. Keep your bottom in the chair when you are sitting." "Be safe" is one of Brooks' four main rules, and "Keep your bottom in the chair when you are sitting" is the specific behavior she wants Abby to do.

Redirect children's behavior. Redirection provides children with an acceptable alternative to the unacceptable behavior they are engaged in. For example, give an infant a rubber toy to chew on when he picks up the piece of paper that was on the floor. Remind a toddler to climb on the climber instead of the table.

Offer two acceptable choices. Choices support a toddler's desire to be independent. They give children some control over what is happening. Make sure that both choices are acceptable to you and reasonable for the child. Do not offer an unrealistic or unacceptable choice, such as, "You may come with me now or you may stay alone on the playground."

> **Barbara** tells Leo (18 months), "You may walk to the door by yourself, or you may hold my hand while we walk to the door together."

Change the environment. This can involve moving a child to a new location. For example, you might gently pick up a baby who is crawling on a rough sidewalk and place him on the grass to crawl. As you do so, explain why you are moving him. Changing the environment can also mean changing something about the child's location. For example, when an infant starts rolling over, you might move some objects out of his way so that he can continue his activity. By observing children carefully, you will be able to determine what additions or changes you need to make to your room to support positive guidance.

Be specific. When you see children behaving appropriately, comment specifically. Rather than simply praising children by saying, "Good job," encourage children by explaining exactly what they are doing and why it is appropriate.

> **Abby** (14 months) hands a cracker to Michael. Brooks says to her, "You are giving Michael a cracker. That makes him happy because he is hungry, too."

Model specific language. Help children who are beginning to speak by giving them the language they need. Telling children to "Use your words" is not helpful to toddlers and twos. They need you to give them the words to use and model how to use them.

> **Matthew** (22 months) grabs a truck from a child who is holding two trucks. Mercedes coaches Matthew. "Say, 'I want a truck too, please.' Now you say it."

It is all right if his version sounds like "Truck, too, p'ease." The important thing is that he is learning to use words to convey his wants and needs.

Say, "When…then…" These statements explain to children the expected sequence of behaviors. It lets them know the appropriate next step.

> **LaToya** says to Jonisha (33 months), "When you put on your shoes, then you may go outside."

Use the "tell and show" strategy. *Tell and show* involves telling children what they should do while showing them by using gestures and other visual cues.

> **Grace** says, "We need to put our coats on before we can go outside," while she holds up the coat for Willard (11 months) to see.

You can also use this strategy to draw children's attention to other people's feelings.

> **Ivan** says to Gena (30 months), "Look at Keisha's face. She is showing you that she doesn't like it when you take her teddy."

Make a reflective statement that begins with "I see…" This shows children that you are paying attention to what they are doing. Simply say exactly what you see happening. Letting children know that you notice them can sometimes be enough to stop challenging behaviors. Reflective statements can also encourage children's play and exploration.

> **LaToya** approaches Valisha (33 months) in the block area, where Valisha has built a structure. LaToya says, "Valisha, I see you have used all of the square blocks. You have stacked them very high."

Say how you feel and why you feel that way. Use "I" statements. Such statements explain to a child what is happening, your feelings about the situation, and the reason for your feelings. They help children understand that their actions affect others. By labeling your own feelings, you help children learn names for feelings and support children's developing ability to empathize with others.

> **Brooks** tells Abby (14 months), "I feel scared when you climb on the shelf, because you could fall and get hurt," as she helps her climb off the shelf.

Use your sense of humor. You can use humor to deflect tension, energize a child, and win his cooperation.

> **Mercedes** makes a silly face and pretends to be a giant by taking large steps, on a day when Matthew (22 months) is whining and walking slowly back from the park.

When you take a positive approach to guiding children's behavior, you help children learn self-control and promote their self-esteem. However, some behaviors challenge your patience or upset you.

Responding to Challenging Behaviors

Physical aggression, temper tantrums, and biting are among the most common challenging behaviors. Many caring teachers struggle to deal with these behaviors every day.

The first step is to try to determine the cause of the behavior. Challenging behaviors are often cries for help. Children who use these behaviors may not know how to express their feelings in other ways. Toddlers and twos may not be able to use verbal language to express their anger or frustration. Focus on what the child needs, rather than on what she is doing. Try to imagine what the child might say if she could. Record your observations.

- What time of day did the behavior occur?
- Who was involved?
- What preceded the unwanted behavior?

As you collect and analyze your observations, you may find a pattern that will help you understand the cause of the behavior. You do not have to handle particularly challenging behaviors on your own. Talk with others who know the child well. A child's family and your co-teachers may have information to help you understand the child. A co-teacher may have noticed a pattern of behavior that you missed. The child's family may know about events at home or in the neighborhood that may be upsetting their child. Talking with families about challenging behaviors allows you to collaborate with them in providing the best care for their child at school and at home.

Physical Aggression

Physical aggression must be stopped immediately, and the victim must be given immediate attention. Intervene by positioning yourself on the aggressive child's level and clearly stating the rule about physical aggression. Involve the child in comforting the one who was hurt (if the hurt child permits this). When a child is physically aggressive and has lost control, you may need to hold her until she calms. Children are frightened when they lose control. Your firm hold can help the child feel safe because you have taken charge of the situation.

When children lose control, you can help them compose themselves by modeling calm behavior. Keep in mind that you cannot help children develop self-control if you are out of control. Screaming at children, isolating them with a time-out system, taking away privileges, and making them feel incompetent rarely produce positive results. **Physical punishment is never, ever acceptable**; neither is using food as a punishment (or reward). Use positive guidance strategies to avoid power struggles with toddlers and twos.

Remember that both the aggressor and the victim need your positive attention. When adults pay too much attention to the victim, the aggressive child feels isolated and guilty, and may continue to be aggressive in order get attention.

Temper Tantrums

Temper tantrums are not fun for anyone. They can leave children feeling exhausted and frightened at their loss of control. They can also make adults feel angry, incompetent, and even embarrassed.

If children could tell us what a tantrum feels like, they would probably describe it as a storm of frustration that sweeps in and overwhelms them. Remember that life can be very frustrating for toddlers and twos. Developmental theory suggests that they are learning about limits. They often struggle to accept the limits you set for them as well as the limits of their own abilities. In addition, they frequently find themselves caught between wanting to be a "big kid" and wanting to be a baby. One minute, they want you to hold them in your arms. The next, they become upset because they cannot put on their own shoes, carry a heavy bag of groceries home from the store, or get you to understand their words verbally.

Once a tantrum begins, there is often little you can do except keep the child from hurting himself or someone else and assure the child that you will help him. After he has calmed down, acknowledge his feelings in ways that show you accept him and his feelings: "Not being able to finish that puzzle really frustrated you! It is scary to be so angry." Suggest other ways to deal with the frustration: "Next time you are frustrated, you can ask me to help you." It is best to focus your energies on preventing tantrums.

Planning ahead to minimize temper tantrums will help avoid what can be a very stressful experience for children and for you. Here are some strategies to minimize their occurrence.

Give toddlers and twos plenty of opportunities to be competent. A competent child is less likely to have tantrums. Invite children to help you with everyday chores, such as setting the table. Offer them many opportunities to make choices about what to play with, wear, and eat. Label shelves with pictures so children can find what they want and help put materials away. Read children's cues to help you understand what they want to communicate and respond accordingly.

Minimize frustrations. Create an environment that is as free of frustration as possible. Set up an interesting, safe space that children can explore freely without constantly having you say, "No." Offer toys, games, and puzzles that match the changing abilities of the children in your care. Always make available familiar materials that children have played with successfully in the past.

Give children a chance to be comforted. Very young children need hugs and cuddles. Offer them when they are needed.

Anticipate children's physical needs. You can often prevent tantrums by doing such things as serving lunch before children get too hungry, helping children take naps before they become overly tired, and giving them a chance to play outdoors when they are ready for active play.

Biting

Biting is very common in groups of young children. It is always upsetting and can be frightening for children, parents, and teachers alike. As with tantrums, focus your energies on prevention. Observe so that you can anticipate when a child might bite, and redirect the child to a more appropriate situation or behavior. Understanding the reasons for biting will help you use effective strategies to prevent the behavior.[26]

Why Children Sometimes Bite	Strategies to Help Prevent Biting
Teething causes their mouths to hurt.	Offer children teething toys to mouth.
They are experimenting. An infant or young child may take an experimental bite to touch and taste other people and learn more about them.	Provide a wide variety of sensorimotor experiences to satisfy their curiosity, such as fingerpainting, playing with dough, preparing and eating food, or engaging in water and sand play.
They are exploring cause and effect, and they want to make something happen. Young children like to have an impact on their world. Biting is a sure way to do so.	Provide different activities and toys that respond to children's actions and help them learn about cause and effect. Show them other ways to affect their world by modeling verbal language.
They are trying to approach or interact with another child.	Give children many opportunities to interact with one another. Guide their behavior as necessary to encourage positive interactions.
They feel frustrated. Some children lack skills to cope with situations and feelings. When frustrated or angry, they bite.	Watch for signs of increasing frustration and potential conflict. You can often prevent harmful incidents by responding to children's needs promptly.
They are overwhelmed by too much noise, confusion, or excitement. Too much going on around them and intense emotion can make children feel out of control.	Be aware when noise, confusion, and excitement begin to escalate to the point that children feel out of control. Calm the situation and individual children as necessary.
They are asking for attention. They know that biting is one way to have people focus on them.	Reinforce positive social behavior. If children get attention when they are not biting, they will not have to use this negative behavior to feel noticed.
They are imitating behavior.	Model loving, supportive behavior. Offer children positive alternatives to negative behavior. **Never bite a child to show how it feels to be bitten.**

Why Children Sometimes Bite	Strategies to Help Prevent Biting
They feel threatened or feel that their possessions are being threatened. When some children feel that they are in danger, they bite in self-defense. When some children feel unable to protect their things, they bite.	Provide support and assurance so that the child recognizes that he and his possessions are safe.
They sense the increasing tension of their teachers and family members. As adults' tension increases, they are not as accessible to children. Children sense a loss of their secure base, and that sense makes them more likely to bite.	Recognize and explain to families that biting is an unfortunate fact of life in group care. Agree on steps you are taking to prevent biting. Help adults see how children quickly pick up their tension, making a bad situation worse.

Unfortunately, no matter how attentive you are, it is likely that a child in your program will bite another child sooner or later. Here are suggestions for that moment.

Respond to the situation promptly. As soon as an incident takes place, you must take immediate action.

- Comfort the child who was bitten.
- Wash the wound. Apply an ice pack to help keep bruising down. If the skin is broken, follow the universal precautions for handling blood, which include wearing nonporous disposable gloves and recommend that both sets of parents notify their pediatrician and follow his or her advice.
- State clearly that biting is not all right. Speak firmly and seriously. However, avoid being overly dramatic to ensure that your response does not make the act of biting more interesting and appealing. Do not use your voice to punish the child by making her feel guilty.
- Invite the child who bit to help you care for the bitten child (unless the child who was bitten seems afraid of the child who bit). This gives the child the opportunity to help and to leave the role of aggressor. Use these moments to offer the biter support and to teach caring behavior. Remember, from the biter's point of view, it is scary to be so out of control that he hurts someone.
- Help the child who bit understand that there are other ways to express anger and frustration, such as using words or growling like a tiger.

Document biting injuries. Include the name of the child who was bitten, as well as the date, time, and location of the incident. Describe how the injury occurred and the actions you took. This information will be helpful in identifying patterns. It will also help you keep the situation in perspective.

Acknowledge your own feelings so you do not add more tension to the situation. Of course you are upset when a child is hurt, but children are quick to notice your feelings. Biting can be particularly frustrating for you, because it can occur despite your preventive measures. Talk with colleagues about biting and help one another maintain emotional balance.

Hold onto your positive vision of the child. When a child is biting, adults tend to focus solely on the negative behavior. They may refer to the child as "The Problem" or even "The Mouth." A child who is biting is a child in distress. He or she needs your care and support.

Make and carry out an ongoing prevention and intervention plan. Here are some positive steps you can take.

- Observe carefully to identify patterns of instances when biting occurs. For example, is the child more likely to bite before lunch? Does the child bite when things get very loud and confusing?
- Ask the child's family about what might be going on at home. Find out if there have been any recent changes. Talk together about how you might help the child stop biting.
- Decide on a plan. For example, if you notice that a child tends to bite when things get hectic, plan to spend extra one-on-one time with her before she is overstimulated.
- Have someone focus on the child who is biting, ideally someone who knows and enjoys the child. This person should be available to the child all day, to provide support, encourage positive behavior, and, of course, to be ready to step in quickly and to keep the child from biting.
- Observe. Keep track of what is happening. Adapt your plan as necessary.

Help parents understand the situation. Because biting can upset all parents in a program, address this issue before it occurs. Discuss with parents the many reasons why children might bite and describe the various preventive steps. Share strategies that families can use at home to prevent and deal with biting. Invite families to share their strategies with you. Always remember that biting the child back "to see what it feels like" is never an option. If biting does occur, talk with parents directly and openly. Acknowledge their feelings. Consider inviting a community health specialist to meet with parents to address health concerns.

Seek help if biting continues or grows more intense. Although a child's biting usually does not continue long, biting sometimes signals that a child needs special assistance. If you become concerned, call in a community resource person, such as a developmental specialist, to help you explore interventions.

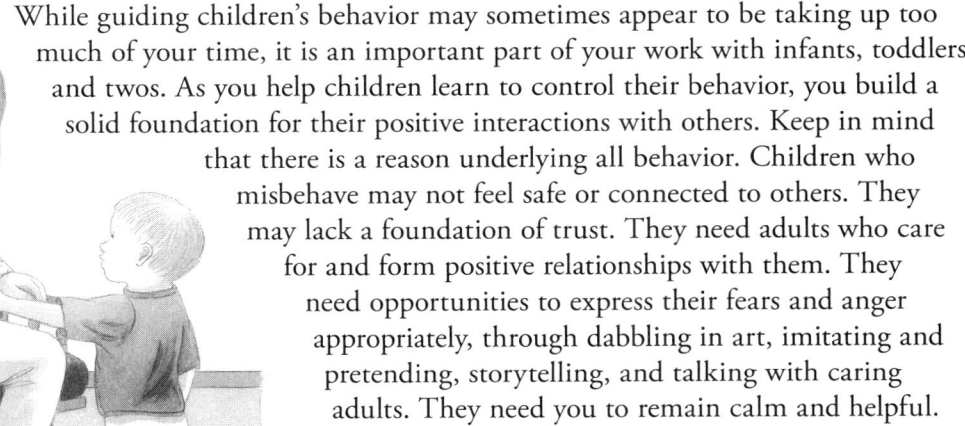

While guiding children's behavior may sometimes appear to be taking up too much of your time, it is an important part of your work with infants, toddlers, and twos. As you help children learn to control their behavior, you build a solid foundation for their positive interactions with others. Keep in mind that there is a reason underlying all behavior. Children who misbehave may not feel safe or connected to others. They may lack a foundation of trust. They need adults who care for and form positive relationships with them. They need opportunities to express their fears and anger appropriately, through dabbling in art, imitating and pretending, storytelling, and talking with caring adults. They need you to remain calm and helpful.

Guiding Children's Learning

Infants, toddlers, and twos are naturally curious. Sometimes they pay attention to what you want them to notice, but sometimes they do not. Sometimes they learn what you intend for them to understand, but they often follow their own interests.

> **Willard** (11 months) is more interested in how the oatmeal box drum rolls down the slide—a lesson in physics—than in playing it during a music experience Grace offered last week. During a walk to a nearby park, **Valisha** and **Jonisha** (33 months) are so interested in the squirrels that they pay little attention to LaToya's suggestion that they collect leaves of various colors.

Working with infants, toddlers, and twos means guiding their learning in ways that let children experience the pleasure, excitement, and sense of competence that accompanies exploration and making discoveries. Positive experiences motivate children to continue learning.

As they engage in routines day after day, children collect, organize, and reorganize information about themselves, other people, and things. That is how they develop understandings that help them make sense of the world. Chapters 6–9 provide extensive information about guiding learning during routines.

In addition to the learning that occurs during daily routines, you promote learning as you offer a variety of experiences to the children in your care.

> **Barbara** notices Leo's (18 months) fascination with the water as he washes his hands. She guides him to the water table, where he can pour water over his hands and arms. That is an experience in exploring sand and water. When **Janet** offers Jasmine a sheet of waxed paper to crumple during lunch and says, "You've crumpled the paper into a ball," she is providing an experience in creating with art.

As children become more skilled, you will offer more planned and more small-group experiences that you initiate and guide. Chapters 11–18 offer ideas about appropriate materials and experiences for young infants, mobile infants, toddlers, and twos.

Learning Through Play

Children play throughout the day during routines and experiences. Their play takes many forms, for example, dropping a spoon off the table again and again, crawling in and out of a cardboard box, exploring the way different fabrics feel, climbing in and out of a chair, and singing a simple song. Play is filled with opportunities for children to develop and learn new skills.

Play offers children opportunities to

- make choices
- make decisions
- solve problems
- interact with one another
- interact with you
- pursue their interests
- experience learning as fun and exciting
- experience themselves as capable, competent, successful learners
- build language and literacy skills, discover mathematical relationships, and be a scientist

Chapter 4: **Caring and Teaching**

As you interact with children throughout the day, think about ways to encourage their efforts and when and how to intervene thoughtfully to support their learning. Follow each child's lead as you decide when to watch, when to step in, and how to lead the child to the next discovery.

> **Julio** (4 months) is reaching for a colorful toy with his right hand. Linda puts a similar toy just within reach of his left hand. **Willard** (11 months) pulls to standing at a cruising rail. Grace encourages him to side step along the railing. **Matthew** (22 months) says, "Me want milk." Mercedes responds, "Oh, you want some more milk. Here it is."

Sometimes, though, the best option is to watch, listen, and give children the time and space to explore on their own. Learning requires attention, time, and practice. In their efforts to help children, teachers sometimes interrupt, distract, and assume control of children's activities. Watching and listening helps ensure that you do not unintentionally interfere with a child's learning. Here are some questions to help you determine when to step in and when to step back.

Are children engaged? If children are focused and busy, your intervention is probably not needed. When children begin moving frequently from toy to toy, wandering aimlessly, or interfering with others' activities, your assistance is required.

Are children stuck? Are they repeating the same activity with little or no variation for an extended time? Young children gain mastery by repeating activities. Yet, when the same activity is repeated in the same way for too long a time, it can be a sign of boredom that may be interfering with learning.

Are there information and skills that require explicit teaching? Sometimes direct teaching makes the most sense.

> **Ivan** shows Gena (30 months) how to sit more steadily by putting her feet on a wooden step. **LaToya** shows Valisha and Jonisha (33 months) how to put on their coats by flipping them over their heads.

Are children in danger? Balance concerns for children's safety with their need to explore. Evaluate whether you frequently say *no* to children in an effort to protect them. While children's safety should never be compromised, children need opportunities to experiment, explore their surroundings, and take reasonable risks.

Talking With Infants, Toddlers, and Twos

Chapter 3, "What Children Are Learning," discusses the importance of promoting children's language and literacy skills. Through the back-and-forth verbal and nonverbal interactions you have with children every day, you help them build their receptive and expressive language skills and learn to have conversations. (You might take turns acting and speaking.) Here are some strategies to use as you talk with children and examples of what you might say when it is your turn to speak.

Describe what a child is seeing or doing: *You dropped the ball, and it rolled onto the rug.*

Verbalize children's emotions: *You are smiling. Digging in the sand makes you happy.*

Use words to show the value you place on learning and problem solving: *You had a good idea. Blowing on the hot noodles makes them cooler.*

Express ideas that children will come to understand over time and with experience: *The dog is barking really loudly.*

Provide vocabulary: *That flower is called a* chrysanthemum. *That word has lots of sounds! Say it with me: chry-san-the-mum.*

Build their confidence as learners: *You are learning where those puzzle pieces go.*

Ask children open-ended questions to extend their thinking. For example,

- To promote exploration: *What do you see, hear, feel?*
- To stretch their thinking about causes and effects: *What do you think will happen if you drop this spoon into the water?*
- To help them think about similarities and differences: *How are these two things the same? Which of these go together?*
- To apply knowledge to solve a problem: *How can we fix the torn page in the book?*

Extending Children's Knowledge and Skills

Each of the children in your group has already acquired knowledge and skills. *Objectives for Development & Learning* will help you identify what each child knows and can do. Building on this base will help children be competent, successful learners. Here are a few suggestions to keep in mind.

Become familiar with the progressions for each objective so you see the next steps in the development of children's knowledge and skills. By pinpointing a child's current levels of development and learning, you can make decisions about how to help him or her progress.

> **Barbara** observes that Leo (18 months) often uses objects in pretend play as they are used in real life (Objective 14, Uses symbols and images to represent something not present; Dimension b, Engages in sociodramatic play). She determines that he appears to be at level 2, Imitates the actions of others; uses real objects as props. To extend his ability to use objects to represent something not present, Barbara offers Leo a block for a pretend cell phone and a cup for a pretend boat when she plays with him.

Balance the familiar with the new and interesting. Small changes or additions to familiar materials and activities enhance children's experiences and often lead to new discoveries and learning.

> **Matthew** (22 months) loves to paint. To give him and others a new experience with painting, Mercedes gives children buckets of water and large brushes to use on the side of the building. This gives Matthew a chance to handle a large brush, make large strokes, and gain a new understanding of the word big.

Plan experiences and interact with children on the basis of what they know and are able to do and what they are ready to try. Offering an enthusiastic word, changing the environment, or gently assisting are ways you can encourage children to something new.

> **Janet** puts out her hands for Jasmine (8 months) to use to pull herself up. She supports Jasmine in her desire to be upright.

Including All Children

All of the children in your care will benefit from the teaching and caring approaches discussed in *The Creative Curriculum*®. Some children will need a little extra support from you because they are learning more than one language or because they have a disability.

Dual-Language Learners

Language learning is an amazing process, and it is even more astonishing when a child under age 3 is learning more than one language. Children may come from a home where they are exposed to two languages. Perhaps one family member speaks to them in Spanish or Chinese, while another always speaks to them in English. Some children hear one language at home and a second language in your program. In both instances, the children are learning two languages at the same time. In simultaneous dual language situations, it is best if each person consistently uses the same language with the child—for example, always Spanish or always English—rather than switching back and forth between the languages.

Children who are learning two languages go through several stages in their learning. Initially, they may mix the languages together, weaving words together from both languages. This use of both languages in one phrase or sentence is called *code-switching*. This stage continues until children are about 30 months old, when they learn to separate the languages, addressing each person with whom they talk in the appropriate language. Children at this stage learn and repeat common phrases that they hear frequently, such as "wanna play," or "gimme the ball." These imitative patterns of speech help children interact with others and are some of the building blocks of language learning.

It is important to support the child's first language in your program, if possible. If some teachers in your program speak the child's home language (other than English), you can adopt the "one person, one language" strategy in which one teacher always speaks the home language while the other always uses English. This strategy is less confusing for children than if each teacher uses multiple languages. It also ensures that children have good language models in each language.

You and your co-teachers should not interpret for each other. For example, when the English-speaking teacher announces that it is time to put on jackets and get ready to go outside, the Spanish-speaking teacher should not repeat the directions in Spanish. Simultaneous interpretation encourages children to ignore English because they know they will soon hear the same information in their primary language. A more effective method is for the teacher to use gestures, body language, and other visual cues that will help the child understand the verbal message. (See chapter 13, "Enjoying Stories and Books," for information about reading books to children who are dual-language learners.)

You can do a number of things if you do not have teachers who speak children's home languages. First, help the child feel comfortable in your program. Communicate nonverbally. Use gestures and simple language. Find out if a family member or other adult who speaks the child's first language can volunteer in your program. Help children know that you value their language by learning caring phrases and common words in the language even if you are not able to speak more of it. Try to provide books and music in the languages of the children in your room. Foster conversations among children in their home languages. Teach English-speaking children some words in another language as well. Assure families that continuing to speak their first language at home will help their children become bilingual.

Children With Disabilities

All children need to be included and successful. Much, if not all, of what you have learned in this chapter can be applied to your work with children who have diagnosed disabilities or other special needs. For this to happen, you must look beyond the specific diagnosis to see what effects it has on a particular child. You must be careful not to generalize about children on the basis of their diagnoses.

See children as children first. Learn about each child's strengths and interests first, and then consider the child's special needs. Use language that reinforces your understanding of this. For example, speak about a child with autism, rather than an autistic child.

Learn about the effects of a specific disability to decide what, if any, adjustments you need to make. For example, a child with a visual impairment relies more heavily on her senses of hearing and touch for communication. When offered choices, it will be helpful for her to touch each item and hear about the choices. A child with a hearing impairment relies heavily on his sense of sight for communication. It may be useful for you to learn sign language and to use cards with pictures of routines, experiences, and materials so that you can communicate with him. A child with a brain injury may need more time to think about what you are saying and to transition from one activity to another. Slowing your conversations and actions may help engage this child. A child with physical limitations needs you to remove physical barriers that might limit her mobility. When you help her move, she will feel respected if you explain what you are doing and why.

Work closely with children's families. The parents of a child with a disability are your greatest sources of support and information. Ask them to share what they know about their child's condition. Invite them also to share tips and strategies they use at home.

> **Gena's** parents helped Ivan learn to position Gena (30 months) in ways that give her the best possible control over her body.

Ask parents about their involvement with the local early intervention program. If they are unaware of local services, give them the necessary information. See chapter 5, "Building Partnerships With Families," for more information about supporting families of children with disabilities.

Set goals and work with a specialist. Use the goals and objectives from a child's Individual Family Service Plan and from *Objectives for Development & Learning* to guide your work with the child. (See chapter 1, "Knowing Infants, Toddlers, and Twos," for more information about this.) Many objectives will be the same as those you have for all children, so many ways of supporting the child will fit easily into your regular planning and daily schedule. For other objectives, you might need to add special toys and adaptive equipment, or you might need to change strategies (such as blinking the lights to catch the attention of a deaf child). These adaptations and strategies should be included in the child's plan. As with all children, you should observe continually and assess the goals and objectives that have been identified, adapting them as necessary. With parental permission, work with the child's specialist(s) to develop strategies that will work in your program.

Encourage, but do not force, appropriate independence. Some children need extra support to develop skills and self-confidence. Competence is important for all children. Recognize, however, that some children may have needs beyond your experience and expertise. If this is the case, seek the help of specialists in your community. Your willingness to learn about various disabilities and reach out to experts will set a good model for the children and adults in your program.

Help children with disabilities engage in play with other children. Remember that sometimes children with disabilities do not initiate play as often as other children. They may need more support to begin playing and more help while they play.

Assessing Children's Development and Learning

Assessment plays a central role in caring and teaching young children. It is an ongoing process of purposefully observing children in order to get to know each child and make decisions about how best to support his or her development and learning.

Assessment is most useful when it is tied closely to curricular objectives. You will find detailed information about the 38 objectives in *Volume 3: Objectives for Development & Learning: Birth Through Kindergarten*. Of course, not all objectives apply to children under 3 years of age. The color-coded system will enable you easily to see which objectives are appropriate for the children in your care. Keeping those objectives in mind will help you observe children purposefully in the context of everyday routines and experiences. You will be able to assess each child's current levels of development and consider next steps. As you learn about each child's strengths and interests, you can use the information and strategies in *The Creative Curriculum®* to build responsive relationships and offer experiences that promote each child's development and learning.

The curricular objectives for development and learning are the same as those of the *Teaching Strategies GOLD™* assessment system. *Teaching Strategies GOLD™* includes the guidance and forms you need for ongoing assessment as you implement *The Creative Curriculum*. If you use a different assessment system, be sure that it is compatible with these objectives. Whatever system you use, there are four steps in the ongoing assessment cycle: (1) observing and collecting facts; (2) analyzing and responding; (3) evaluating; and (4) summarizing, planning, and communicating.

Step 1. Observing and Collecting Facts

In your work, you observe young children every day. You watch what they do, listen to what they say, and decide how to respond. This process happens so quickly, you may not even be aware of its importance. Ongoing observation is an essential part of caring for and teaching young children. When you observe to find out what is unique and special about each child, you have a basis for building a positive relationship and for planning experiences that will enable each child to flourish. To help you remember and use what you learn from your observations, you need to set up a system that works for you.

Setting Up a System

A system is an organized way of keeping track of your observations, making sure that you are documenting each child's development and learning, and, as children get older, storing samples of their work. If you are using *Teaching Strategies GOLD™*, the system for organizing and storing observations notes and digital samples of children's work is already set up. Each child has a *Child Assessment Portfolio* for storing information online or on paper. If you are using another assessment system, you can organize a notebook by each child's name. Samples of children's work can be stored in large envelopes, clean pizza boxes, cardboard magazine holders, accordion files, or hanging files. You may also need a system to name and organize digital photos as well as audio- and video clips.

Because observation is your method for learning what each child knows and can do, you need ways to record what you see and hear. It is best to make basic notes while or immediately after you observe, so you will want to have some convenient ways to do so. You can add more detail to your notes later. Here are some ideas for recording your observations:

- Use mailing labels or sticky notes to write what you see and hear. You can easily transfer them to the child's portfolio.
- Keep sticky notes or file cards in your pocket or readily accessible in different areas of the room.
- Use a digital pen to write notes if you are using an online assessment system that includes this feature. Some pens even have voice recorders so you can interact with a child while the pen is recording.
- Develop your own system of shorthand to record brief notes and phrases that will help you recall what happened.

Documenting Your Observations

Observation notes are most accurate and useful when they are objective and factual. When your notes include words like *shy, aggressive, upset, hyperactive,* or *angry,* they reveal your impressions, interpretations, or assumptions rather than the facts about what a child did or said. Judgmental words may or may not tell an accurate story. Interpretations, impressions, or assumptions include

- labels (e.g., *frustrated, vivacious, creative*)
- intentions (e.g., *wants to*)
- evaluations and judgments (e.g., *good job, beautiful, sloppy*)
- negatives (e.g., *didn't, can't, won't*)

Objective notes include only the facts about what you see and hear. Factual observations include

- descriptions of an action
- quotations of language
- descriptions of a gesture
- descriptions of a facial expression
- descriptions of a creation

Compare the following two examples of observation notes about an infant.

Example 1

Jasmine is being so fussy and manipulative. Every time I put her down, she starts crying again to get her way.

Example 1 is not an objective note. It uses labels (*fussy* and *manipulative*) and includes an intention (*to get her way*).

Now consider another note about the same behavior.

Example 2

Jasmine cries loudly after her mother leaves. She gradually stops crying when I hold her and we sit in the glider, looking at a book together.

Example 2 is an objective note. It includes only the facts about what Jasmine did (*cries loudly after her mother leaves*) and what happened (*stops crying when I hold her and we sit in the glider looking at a book together*). Accurate notes include all the facts about what a child did and said, in the order that they happened.

Writing objective notes takes practice. The more aware you are of what objective notes are like, the more skilled you will become at writing them.

Here are two examples of objective observation notes.

Valisha—9/8

V picks up scissors; begins to cut paper. Moves scissor blades back and forth. Can't get paper to cut; scissors crumples paper. V frowns and drops scissors on table. She looks at Jonisha, who is tearing paper. Picks up her paper and begins tearing it with hands.

Willard—10/30

Crawls to bookshelf. Puts both hands on shelf; pulls himself to standing. Pulls two books off shelf. Turns around and looks at me. I shake my head, "No." Then W lowers himself to floor and crawls to nearby truck.

Other Forms of Documentation

In addition to observation notes, documentation can take many different forms. Here are some examples:

Photographs—Take pictures that show that illustrate what a child can do (e.g., building a block tower, painting, or successfully feeding herself with a spoon). Be sure to label and date each photo and write a brief description of what the child did and said.

Audio- and video clips—Try to record activities without intruding on what children are doing. Be selective about what you record.

Samples of children's work—Select similar samples such as drawings and attempts to write, and collect them over time (e.g., at the beginning, middle, and toward the end of the year).

Checklists, participation lists, frequency counts—Systematically record such things as the types of materials the child chooses, physical skills, response to story reading, and so on.

Observing With the Curricular Objectives in Mind

The objectives for children's development and learning, which are introduced in chapters 1 and 3 and described in detail in *Volume 3,* are a guide for making the observation process systematic and meaningful. You are more likely to collect objective, factual observation notes if you are familiar with the objectives and the particular indicators of the widely held expectations for the children you are observing. Focus your notes on the information you will need later when you are ready to evaluate progress. For example, instead of recording, "Counts crackers at snack time," a more valuable note would be, "Says, 'One, two, seven, five, ten,' as she touched each of the five crackers in front of her." Keep some file cards or sticky notes handy so you can record what you see and hear immediately as you observe children throughout the day.

This volume includes a list of the 38 objectives for development and learning. Keep it handy so you can refer to it often. You can also obtain from Teaching Strategies a colorful poster that shows the objectives at a glance. Displaying it in your classroom will help you as you observe children, and it will help family members understand what their children are learning.

Keep in mind that you do not have to write an observation note about every child, every day. However, do try to select a few children to observe each day. For some objectives, it is sufficient to see a child use a skill once or twice (e.g., a physical skill). You may record such accomplishments on a checklist; an observation note is not usually necessary. Other objectives require more evidence and documentation. No predetermined number of observation notes or amount of other documentation is required for each objective. Use common sense to decide what is needed.

Step 2. Analyzing and Responding

The information you gain by observing children and thinking about their skills is the basis for responding to each child and supporting each child's learning appropriately. Knowing what a child can do in relation to the objectives will tell you such things as whether a child can follow simple directions, how well a child plays with others, and a child's levels of curiosity and persistence. All of this information will help you decide what experiences will interest and challenge children rather than frustrate them.

This step in the assessment cycle involves organizing your documentation and making judgments about what the information tells you about a child's progress in terms of the objectives. As you observe children or review your notes, ask yourself, "What does this behavior mean?" When you can find time, systematically organize your notes and reflect on what you are learning. At other times, it is appropriate to respond immediately.

To analyze the documentation you have collected, review your notes and samples of work and think about which objectives apply to each item. Record the objective numbers directly on your notes or samples of work. Keep in mind that one rich observation note can relate to several different objectives. Regularly ask yourself, "What does this observation tell me about the child's development and learning?" Using *Objectives for Development & Learning*, here is how you might analyze the sample observation notes that were presented earlier.

The observation note about Valisha is clearly related to Objective 7, *Demonstrates basic fine-motor strength and coordination.* You would write *7* on the note and place it on the appropriate page in Valisha's *Child Assessment Portfolio* or enter it online. The observation note also gives information about Valisha's social–emotional development, particularly about Objective 1, *Regulates own emotions and behaviors*, and Objective 11, *Demonstrates positive approaches to learning*. You may want to make a copy of the note to put on the pages for those objectives. If you are using the online system, simply select multiple related objectives after entering the documentation.

The observation note about Willard also provides information about at least three objectives. It gives you information about Objective 4, *Demonstrates traveling skills*; Objective 1, *Regulates own emotions and behaviors*, and Objective 8, *Listens to and understands increasingly complex language*.

Valisha—9/8

V picks up scissors; begins to cut paper. Moves scissor blades back and forth. Can't get paper to cut; scissors crumples paper. V frowns and drops scissors on table. She looks at Jonisha, who is tearing paper. Picks up her paper and begins tearing it with hands.

7, 1, 11

Willard—10/30

Crawls to bookshelf. Puts both hands on shelf; pulls himself to standing. Pulls two books off shelf. Turns around and looks at me. I shake my head, "No." Then W lowers himself to floor and crawls to nearby truck.

4, 1, 8

In your daily work with children, you continually observe, reflect on what you see, and respond to each child. You respond in the moment and later use what you learn when planning experiences that will extend children's learning. In each of the chapters on routines and experiences, you will find charts with examples of how to observe, analyze, and respond to children throughout the day, keeping the objectives in mind.

Step 3: Evaluating Each Child's Progress

Evaluating children's progress means thinking about all of the objectives and deciding which level a child has reached on each of the applicable objectives. *Volume 3: Objectives for Development & Learning* shows the developmental progression for each objective so you can pinpoint a child's level. The colored bands show the reasonable expectations for the development and learning of children in each age-group. Start with the level appropriate for the child's age and decide which of the indicators best describes the child's skill level for the objective. Consider all the documentation you have collected.

To understand the evaluation process, consider the observation note about Willard that was presented previously. This note gives you information about Objective 1, *Regulates own emotions and behaviors*. The note reminds you that Willard looked at you after taking books from the shelf. He did not pull more books off the shelf after you shook your head, "No." Three dimensions of Objective 1 address its several aspects. The one that applies to this observation is Dimension b, *Follows limits and expectations*.

b. Follows limits and expectations

Not Yet	1	2	3	4	5	6	7	8	9
		Responds to changes in an adult's tone of voice and expression • Looks when adult speaks in a soothing voice • Appears anxious if voices are loud or unfamiliar • Touches the puddle of water when adult smiles encouragingly		**Accepts redirection from adults** • Moves to the sand table at suggestion of adult when there are too many at the art table • Initially refuses to go inside, but complies when the teacher restates the request		**Manages classroom rules, routines, and transitions with occasional reminders** • Indicates that only four people may play at the water table • Cleans up when music is played • Goes to rest area when lights are dimmed		**Applies rules in new but similar situations** • Walks and uses a quiet voice in the library • Runs and shouts when on a field trip to the park • Listens attentively to a guest speaker	

On the basis of this one observation note, you may decide that Willard shows evidence of being at levels 2 and 4. You would not make a final determination about Willard's level on the basis of this single observation. However, you can make a preliminary determination that Willard is at level 3 and continue to collect more information before you finalize your decision. Summarizing the child's progress is the next step in the assessment cycle.

Step 4: Summarizing, Planning, and Communicating

This last step in the assessment cycle involves summarizing what you know about each child, developing plans for individual children and the group, and communicating your findings to families and others to whom you report. With assessment information, you can plan routines, transitions, and experiences, and change the environment appropriately.

Summarizing

Three or four times during the year, you identify the levels each child has reached for the various objectives and dimensions. Then you summarize the child's development and learning. If you are using the *Teaching Strategies GOLD*™ assessment system, you can use the forms designed for that purpose. Teachers who use a different assessment system also need a way to summarize the information they have collected and to prepare reports.

Objectives for Development & Learning explains widely held expectations for children birth through kindergarten. It can be used with all children, those developing according to expectations and those who are advanced, have a developmental delay, have a disability, or lack experience in an area. You should not expect every child in your program to progress to the highest levels for each objective. Over the course of the year, however, you would hope to see evidence that every child is making some degree of progress.

Planning

The wealth of information you have about each child is only meaningful if you link it to decisions about how best to support the child's development and learning. You use this information to plan for children individually and for your group as a whole. In chapter 2, we discussed the "Child Planning Form" and the "Group Planning Form." The information you collect about each child is extremely important to using these planning forms.

Here are some examples of how the assessment information about individual children informs a teacher's planning.

Jasmine (8 months) is delighted with her new ability to crawl around the room (Objective 4, *Demonstrates traveling skills*). Janet wants to encourage her to crawl safely wherever Jasmine wants to go. She makes some changes in the physical environment to block off areas that are not safe and give Jasmine plenty of room to roam on her own.

Mercedes has documented a number of examples where Mathew (22 months) began classifying objects (Objective 13, *Uses classification skills*). He helped her find all the cars and put them in the basket at cleanup time, and he picked out all the red pegs to place on the large peg board. On the basis of these observations, Mercedes determines that Mathew is beginning to match simple objects (level 1). To encourage this skill, Mercedes decides to bring out some new classification toys for the toy area, and she will interact with the children as they use them.

Ivan has noted that Gena (30 months) enjoys the songs and fingerplays he sings with the children (Objective 15, *Demonstrates phonological awareness*; Dimension a, *Notices and discriminates rhyme*). His careful observations tell him that Gena joins in rhyming songs and games (level 2), but she rarely fills in the missing rhyme or generates rhyming words. Choosing among the strategies presented in *Volume 3: Objectives for Development & Learning* for supporting children's development and learning in relation to Objective 15, Ivan plans to focus on having Gena and the other children fill in rhyming words. He includes specific songs and rhymes as he completes a "Group Planning Form."

Communicating

The progress of the children in your group is of interest to others as well as to you. Families want to know how their children are doing, and they have valuable information to share. In many programs, administrators want to review reports, and some funders require reports to verify that their investments are leading to positive results.

Most programs schedule conferences with children's families several times during the year. It is important to prepare for these conferences and to have a form on which to summarize the information you want to share with families. The "Family Conference Form" that is provided in the Appendix of this volume and that is part of the *Teaching Strategies GOLD*™ assessment system serves that purpose. Review the samples of the child's work and the child's level of development for each of the objectives. Think about what information and evidence is most important to the child's family in each of the areas of development and learning. Write a brief description of the child's strengths and give examples of what the child can do in each area. Identify a few learning goals you have in mind for the child. In chapter 5, we discuss how to prepare for and conduct family conferences.

If you are using the online system for *Teaching Strategies GOLD*™, the process of creating reports is streamlined for you. Data about the objectives can be aggregated and disaggregated for a range of individual and group reports.

Conclusion

The essence of caring for and teaching infants, toddlers, and twos is building a responsive and caring relationship with each child. Appreciating and finding joy in the everyday discoveries that delight a child are what make your work so satisfying and enjoyable. As you observe and get to know each child, you reflect and respond to his strengths, needs, and interests; purposefully guide his behavior; support his learning; and use ongoing assessment to document his progress and to plan. Families are your partners in caring for and teaching infants, toddlers, and twos. We turn to this topic in the next chapter.

Building Partnerships With Families

Special Concerns of Families With Children Under Age 3	**142**
The Stress of Parenting an Infant	142
Conflicting Feelings About Sharing Care	143
Wanting to Be Part of Their Child's Day	143
Getting to Know Families	**144**
Appreciating Differences Among Families	144
Understanding the Influence of Culture	145
Welcoming Families to Your Program	**146**
Creating a Welcoming Environment	146
Orienting New Families	147
Developing an Individual Care Plan for Each Child	148
Reaching Out to All Family Members	149
Communicating With Families	**150**
Building Trust Through Daily Interactions	150
Making the Most of Daily Exchanges	152
Communicating in More Formal Ways	154
Holding Conferences With Families	155
Making Home Visits	157
Involving Families in the Program	**158**
Offering a Variety of Ways to Be Involved	158
Participating in the Program	160
Sharing Information and Parenting Tips	**161**
Responding to Challenging Situations	**162**
Resolving Differences: A Partnership Approach	162
Working Through Conflicts	165
Supporting Families Who Are Under Stress	169
Supporting the Families of Children With Disabilities	171

Building Partnerships With Families

Very young children come to your program with their families. To serve them well, you must develop meaningful partnerships with their families. In a true partnership, families and caregivers bring equal value to the relationship, and they do so to benefit the child.

Taking care of children under age 3 means that you are *sharing the care* with families. The issues you must discuss and agree upon with families are rooted in strong beliefs and practices. The partnership you create together is an essential factor in how infants, toddlers, and twos experience child care and how much they gain from the experience.

This chapter explains the fifth component of *The Creative Curriculum® for Infants, Toddlers & Twos* and offers practical ideas for working with families to develop partnerships based on trust and mutual respect. It has six sections:

Special Concerns of Families With Children Under Age 3 discusses the stress of parenting an infant, conflicting feelings about sharing care, and the desire of family members to be part of their child's day.

Getting to Know Families explores differences between families and the influence of culture upon child-rearing practices.

Welcoming Families to Your Program suggests ways to create a welcoming environment and to orient new families to the program. It also explains how to develop an *Individual Care Plan* and the importance of reaching out to all family members.

Communicating With Families show how mutual trust is built through daily interactions with families. It suggests ways to make the most of daily exchanges, more formal communication, conferences, and home visits.

Involving Families in the Program explains a variety of ways to encourage the involvement and participation of family members.

Responding to Challenging Situations presents a partnership approach to resolving differences with families, working through conflicts, supporting families who are under stress, and assisting the families of children with disabilities.

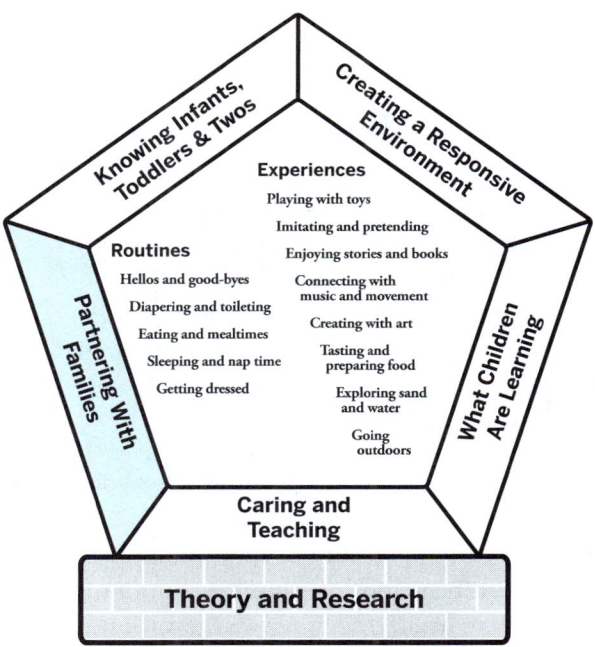

Special Concerns of Families With Children Under Age 3

Think about what it means for new parents to be considering your program for their infant, toddler, or 2-year-old. If they put their thoughts into words, they might ask you these questions:

Will my child…

- be safe and free from harm?
- receive a lot of attention?
- feel comfortable and happy in this child care program?
- be with adults who are warm, loving, and responsive?
- still love me best?
- miss me when we are apart?
- have interesting things to see and to do?
- learn to get along with other children?
- hear lots of language?
- be with adults who know and respect our family?

These questions reflect the uncertainties and fears that parents often experience when they seek child care for their infant, toddler, or 2-year-old. Everything you do to assure families that you and your program will respond positively to their concerns will encourage the trust and confidence essential to building a partnership. Begin by thinking about what parents are feeling during this exciting but vulnerable period of their lives.

The Stress of Parenting an Infant

Being the parent of an infant takes energy. Not only are new parents often confused by their child's behavior and unsure of what to do, but they are also very, very tired. Lack of sleep makes it easy for new parents to lose perspective and to despair that they can ever learn as much as they need to know. When a parent is very young, single, or worried about having enough money to provide essentials, the tension is significant. The stress that parents experience as they prepare for a day of work, get their children ready for the day, and cope with traffic is a major challenge. They sometimes arrive at child care feeling anxious and exhausted.

Some families are comfortable about sharing their feelings and asking you for the support they need. Others are not. They may be too overwhelmed with the changes in their lives. They might not yet trust you, or they might view asking for help as a sign of failure. You can be helpful because you communicate with families every day. If you listen carefully, you may be able to figure out how best to offer help. For example, sometimes your help will be to reassure parents that what they are experiencing is very common and that things will become easier. Sometimes you will offer parents places to sit and read with their children before leaving for work.

Conflicting Feelings About Sharing Care

Placing an infant, toddler, or 2-year-old in a child care program often involves conflicting feelings. Some parents feel relieved when they find a high-quality child care program with a professional and trustworthy staff. At the same time, it is not unusual for new parents to feel sorrow, guilt, or even fear about sharing the care of their child with people they do not know well. They may regret their need to return to work and worry about all they will miss each day. They may even worry that their child will like you better than she likes them. These feelings can be stressful for parents.

You may also have mixed feelings about sharing care. Because working with infants, toddlers, and twos is such passionate work, it is natural to feel deeply protective and attached to young children. You may begin to feel a bit competitive with a parent.

Parents and teachers each play an important but different role in a child's life. Children know who is who. Parents are the most important people to a child. Their relationship is forever. It is built upon a deep trust and a love unlike any other. No matter how skilled and experienced you are, you can never take the place of a parent.

With these conflicting feelings in mind, you can understand how vital it is to reassure parents who have young children in child care that they are the most important people in their child's life and that their role is primary.

Wanting to Be Part of Their Child's Day

Children change so quickly during their first 3 years that many parents wonder if they will miss important events in their child's life. For this reason, the conversations you have with their families are often personal and intense. You can expect them to want to know all that happens during the time their children are in your care. They want details about what and how much they ate, how well they slept, when they had diaper changes, what toys they played with, and how they related to other children and adults.

However, there is one major exception to your need to share information. No one wants to miss one of his child's "firsts." For example, if you see the first time a child sits up or takes first steps, you may not want to share this information fully. Instead, consider saying something like this: "Tyrone pulled himself up a lot today! I have a feeling that he is about to take his first step. I'll be curious to know what happens over the weekend. I'm going to remember to ask you on Monday morning." Then write yourself a note so you do not forget to ask what happened.

Getting to Know Families

Just as you get to know each child and use what you learn to build a relationship, you begin building partnerships with families by getting to know the most important people in each child's life. By being familiar with the unique characteristics, strengths, and issues important to each family, you can find ways to build the necessary trust and respect. Begin by recognizing the many ways families differ and the profound influence of each family's culture.

Appreciating Differences Among Families

Every family is different. The traditional family—two parents and their children—is not as common as it once was. Many children are growing up with one parent. Some are being reared by grandparents or other relatives. Other children live with two mothers or two fathers. To appreciate differences among the families you serve, start by keeping an open mind about what constitutes a family. Remember, to children, their families are the most important people in the world.

Some families are easy to get to know. They are open to meeting new people, feel comfortable in a new environment, and they are eager to communicate with you about their child and the program. Others are uneasy and unsure of themselves. This may be their first experience using child care and they do not know what to expect, or they may have had a negative experience with child care in the past. Their communication style may differ from yours. For example, they may be uncomfortable with direct questions and reluctant to answer them. They may view you as an authority figure and wonder why you are asking for their advice when you are the expert. Try to understand these differences and not to assume that the same approach will work with each family.

Families bring a wide range of life experiences that shape who they are and how they relate to others. The level of education that family members have achieved, socioeconomic status, health issues, and length of time in this country also account for differences among families. Some are new parents and are very young. Others are caring for elderly or ill family members as well as their infant. Some are facing challenging circumstances such as unemployment, substance abuse, low literacy skills, unstable or unsafe housing, depression, or lack of access to a phone or transportation. Others are experiencing long separations from loved ones who are away for military service or in prison. You may have families who have only recently come to this country, do not know the language, and are trying to understand how to fit in. They may expect to be here permanently or plan to return to their country of origin.

The parents in your program may have jobs that are very demanding. They may be struggling to balance the demands of work and finding that they have little time for their child. Your sensitivity to these different life circumstances influence how families relate to you, and it can help you build the partnerships that are essential to providing high-quality care.

Understanding the Influence of Culture

Culture involves the customary beliefs, values, and practices people learn from their families and communities, either through example (watching what others do) or through explicit instruction (being told what is expected). Cultural background affects how people communicate and interact with others, and it shapes their expectations of how others will respond. Because every culture has its own set of rules and expectations, different cultures interpret what people do and say differently. Culture has a very strong influence on child-rearing practices, beliefs, and goals. Your belief system was probably influenced by those directly responsible for rearing you. Think about your own beliefs and how they influence your practice.

It will help you to learn as much as possible about the different cultures of the families in your program, keeping in mind that every family is different. Try not to generalize about any group's characteristics. Consider the many factors that influence the practices and values of an individual family, including the family's country of origin, its social class there and here, the parents' educational background, and whether extended family members live in the home.

It is easy to misinterpret what families do or say if you do not understand something about their culture. However, you also must avoid assigning cultural labels to families. Rather than making assumptions about cultural influences, it is better to keep an open mind and consider the values behind each family's beliefs. Seek to discover answers to questions such as those that follow, keeping in mind that not all families will be comfortable responding to direct questions.

Observe how family members interact with their child, and be selective about the kinds of questions you ask each family.

- Who are the people in the child's immediate family?
- Who are the decision makers in the family? Are decisions made by one person or several people?
- Do all family members live in the same household?
- Who is the primary caregiver of young children in the family?
- How are children's names chosen?
- How does the family balance children's independence with doing things for them?
- When should toilet learning begin, and how should it be handled?
- What, when, and how are children fed?
- How is discipline handled?
- Do family members have different and distinct roles in rearing children?
- Are boys and girls treated differently?
- Is it acceptable for children to be noisy and to get dirty?
- What kinds of questions are children asked?
- How do adults respond to children's questions?
- How do people interact with one another? Do they look each other in the eye? Are they taught to pause and think carefully about a response before giving it? Do they touch each other as they communicate?
- How do families show respect for elders? For children?

Welcoming Families to Your Program

To develop partnerships with families, take the time to help all families feel comfortable and respected in the program setting. You can create a welcoming environment by thoughtfully organizing spaces and materials. Your initial contacts with families are the first opportunities to begin to get to know them and to learn from them. By involving families in developing a plan for their child, you show that you are sharing the care of their child and that their ideas are invaluable. Remember to think about the possible need to reach out to multiple members of a child's family.

Creating a Welcoming Environment

Your program's environment conveys messages to families. It can say, "Leave your child with us. We're in charge here," or it can say, "We care for your child together. You are always welcome here." Look around as if you were a parent. Does the physical environment welcome families and invite them to participate in the program? Here are some ideas to consider.

Make the **entranceway** attractive, neat, and inviting. Include items such as plants, photographs of the children with their families, and displays of children's work. Arrange space near children's cubbies where family members can undress and dress a child and sit together briefly before saying good-bye. A place that says, "Saying good-bye can be difficult; take your time," helps to ease the transition from home to your room.

Provide a **mail/message box** for each family. To help you sort messages easily by language, color code the mailboxes according to the home languages of the families. This practice will make it easy to put the messages in the right place. Do not assume, however, that every family wants to receive messages in their home language. Although their home language might not be English, the family may want to receive messages in English.

Post a whiteboard at the entrance to your room and write a daily message about what happened that day.

Keep a **bulletin board** with up-to-date information about program activities, upcoming meetings, and community events that are of interest to families.

Display **objects that families have brought** for the children to explore, such as handmade quilts, weavings, musical instruments, photos, cooking tools, and ceremonial items.

Mount an attractive display of **photographs** of the children in your class and their families. Either put them on the wall where children can see them or place them in durable photo books that can be handled by the children.

Offer **books and pictures** for children that honor the diversity of the families who are served by your program.

Provide **places for family members** to hang their coats and store their belongings during their visits. Be sure that purses and tote bags are stored out of children's reach, because they often contain unsafe items.

Place a comfortable **rocking chair or glider** in a private space where mothers can nurse their babies. Be cautious about using a rocking chair in an area where crawling infants might injure their fingers.

Offer easily accessed **resources** that parents may read and check out. Juggling daily transitions from home to your room with small children is a challenge. When resources are readily available to families, it is more likely they will use and benefit from them. Locate them inside your room, just outside your door, or at the entrance to the building.

Place a **suggestion box** in a prominent place and provide slips of paper and pens. Be sure to take time to read the suggestions and follow up.

Orienting New Families

Initial contacts with children's families are opportunities to begin building partnerships. Welcome families, introduce your program, and get to know a little about each child and his family members. Depending on your program's procedures, your first contact with families may be at enrollment.

The program director or a parent liaison usually makes the initial contacts with parents, but sometimes teachers are asked to help with enrollment and orientation. Think about what will make families feel comfortable from the start. How can you convey that you are eager to get to know them and their child? Ask yourself whether it is appropriate to serve something to eat or drink. Do you need to arrange for someone who speaks the family's home language to be present?

Collect items to give and list things to do to orient families to the program:

- enrollment form
- health history or medical form
- "Individual Care Plan—Family Information Form"
- brochure, flyer, or handbook
- tour the facility and introduce staff members
- schedule a transition visit for the child, family members, and primary teacher

An enrollment form with specific questions about the child's history and about the family is one way to gather information. Explain how the information requested on the form will be helpful to all staff members who will care for the child. Open-ended questions will help you begin to learn about the child and family.

- What would you most like us to know about your child?
- How is your child comforted best?
- What does your child enjoy doing?
- What are your hopes and dreams for your child?
- What do you most want your child to learn in our program?
- Are there any special traditions, celebrations, stories, or songs that are especially important to your family and your child?
- Are there any special concerns that we should know about as we care for your child?
- How would you like to participate in the program?

A brochure or flyer with some of the basic information that family members need to know is helpful. Some programs give each family a booklet that introduces the program's philosophy and goals for children, describes the kinds of experiences children will have, and outlines policies and procedures.

A transition meeting or home visit before the child begins coming on a regular basis is important for you, the family, and the child. Such a visit helps all of you begin to get to know one another. Visiting the program gives the family and child a chance to become familiar with the new surroundings. As you watch the child interacting with a familiar person, you will learn how to make the child feel comfortable. As you chat with the family, you gain information for the Individual Care Plan that is explained in the next section.

As you converse with each family, find out what language the child hears at home. If it is not a language you speak, ask the family to help you learn a few words so you can use them with their child.

You might also use these initial meetings to begin sharing information about child development, routines, experiences, and the curriculum. When the child begins coming to the program, encourage a family member to plan to stay for a while, to help the child feel comfortable with you.

Developing an Individual Care Plan for Each Child

The people involved in a partnership share responsibility and the power to influence what happens. In your program, you share the care of each child. You and the child's family have different but important roles to play, as well as the skills and knowledge needed to plan for the child's experiences in child care.

An Individual Care Plan (ICP) summarizes information about how best to handle daily routines for an individual child. It helps you care for each child in ways that are consistent with the child's home experiences. The plan is developed *with* the family when the child enters your program, and it is updated as the child's care patterns change. Developing an

ICP with the child's family lets them know that you intend to share the care of their child. It also sends the message that you recognize families as experts on their children and that you want to benefit from their knowledge. A sample form for writing an ICP is included in the Appendix. Keep the ICP form where it is accessible to everyone who cares for the child, including substitute teachers.

In order to develop an ICP, you need detailed information about how the child is cared for at home. "The Individual Care Plan—Family Information Form" (see the Appendix) includes questions about arrival and departure times, breast-feeding or bottle-feeding, food preferences and allergies, diapering or toileting needs, and sleeping habits. It will help you get the information you need to collect by talking with the child's family. Use the information to complete the child's "Individual Care Plan" form.

> **Julio** (4 months) will enter the program tomorrow. At the transition meeting today, Maria, his mother, shares information with Linda about his sleeping patterns. Linda learns that Julio is a fitful sleeper. He likes to be rocked to sleep, loud noises startle him, and singing soothes him. Linda listens, asks questions, and then records Maria's responses on the "Individual Care Plan—Family Information Form." She collects information about Julio's preferences, and she will accommodate them as much as possible in the child care environment.

Reaching Out to All Family Members

Parents are not the only family members who should feel welcome in your program. Other members of a child's family may be sharing the care of the child and might want to be involved in the program. Grandparents, for example, might have more free time to share than parents and may have a great deal of patience with young children. Their participation in the program is valuable; they can feed an infant, read to a child, play games and sing, help a child settle for a nap, and more.

Identify special projects or events that interest different family members. For example, you might invite grandparents or special friends to read or tell stories and invite those interested in construction projects to help with a "fix-it" day. Ask family members about topics of interest to them and arrange special speakers or activities.

You might need to make a special effort to welcome and involve fathers, who sometimes feel uncomfortable in an early childhood setting where more women are involved than men. Once fathers discover that their presence and their contributions are appreciated by the program staff and are important to their child, they are more likely to take an active role. By *father* we do not necessarily mean only the child's biological father. A father figure may be another significant male who is a steady influence in the child's life: the mother's partner or husband, an uncle, older sibling, grandfather, another relative, or a family friend.

The most important thing to keep in mind is that all children need caring adults in their lives who take an interest in their development and learning. Find out which adults are important in a child's life and think about how you can welcome them. Learn about their interests, jobs, hobbies, and what they would like to share with the children. Describe what others have contributed to the program. Some adults are more likely to participate in an activity that involves the whole family than in one that is designed solely for parents.

Communicating With Families

Good communication is essential to partnerships. Families want to know all the details about their children's experiences during the day, everything from what and how much they ate to what and with whom they played and how they reacted to experiences. Families often have information to share as well. Informal daily exchanges are just as valuable as the more formal methods you use to communicate with families. You may need to use several different forms of communication, especially if a child lives in more than one home or has a noncustodial adult who wants to be fully involved.

Building Trust Through Daily Interactions

Every day that a child is in your care, you have opportunities to interact with family members and build the trust that is essential to a partnership. Trust develops only over time and is based on many positive and respectful experiences.

Here are some of the positive messages you can convey to families through your daily interactions.

Message to Families	Daily Interactions
You are always welcome here.	Greet each family member and child by name and say something positive about the child, the family, or the program. Learn at least a few words in the family's home language to use when you talk with the child. (Be aware that some family members might not want you to address them in their home language if you only know a few words of greeting.)
We can learn from you.	Acknowledge the insights and information parents have about their child and how valuable these are to you and other staff members who care for the child.
You are entitled to know what is happening in the program.	Set up systems, such as journals or daily notes, to share what has happened each day. Use simple language and translate the information if necessary. Avoid the use of jargon in both written and spoken communication.
We will share the care of your child.	Complete the *Individual Care Plan—Family Information Form* with the family of each infant and update it regularly. Communicate daily with parents or other family members about their child. Use daily logs to share information about each child's day and hold daily conversations, either in person or by phone.
We can work together to resolve differences and conflicts.	View differences as opportunities to learn more about the family's views and work toward a better understanding. Use the steps for handling conflicts (discussed later in this chapter) to support your partnership.

Every positive interaction you have with a family member builds trust. If you do need to discuss a difficult issue at some time, it will be easier and more productive if you have already built a positive relationship with the family.

Making the Most of Daily Exchanges

When you are caring for very young children, daily exchanges are the primary way to communicate with family members and keep everyone informed about what is happening at home and at the program. Respectful and sincere interactions between families and teachers show children that home and the program are connected. Here are some suggestions for daily exchanges with families.

Greet each child and family personally. Use their names; observe indications of how they are faring, and say something specific about the child, the family, or your plans for the day.

Share information about something the child has accomplished or about an event that concerns the child. News can be shared in the morning, but the end of the day is often a good time to talk with families about what their child has done and to explain its significance. "Let me tell you about the building Janelle made with our blocks yesterday. The way she solved the balancing problem was pretty amazing. She tried several ways of stacking the blocks so they wouldn't fall down." However, leave the announcement of important "firsts" to the parent and child.

Solicit their insights and advice about their child. "I can see that Parker doesn't want to say good-bye to you today. Can you think of any particular reason?"

Give support to families when needed. "Perhaps Maya just needs an extra hug. I know she'll be fine once she gets busy. We have lots planned for today."

Be a good listener. Active listening skills convey that parents' concerns and ideas are taken seriously. "I understand how upset you are about the biting incident. I can assure you that we are taking steps to prevent more biting."

Make sure you understand what is being said. If there is uncertainty about a family member's statement, clarify your understanding. "Tell me whether I understand what you are saying. I think I heard you say. . ."

In communicating with families, try to be specific and factual. Vague or subjective comments can leave family members uncertain about what you mean or make them defensive. Notice the difference between the subjective and objective comments in the two examples that follow. Think about how the parent might feel in each case.

Subjective Comments	Parent's Thoughts
When Julio's mother, Maria, comes to get him at the end of the day, Linda tells her, "Julio was very crabby today. He fussed with everyone who tried to comfort him."	What did he do? How did Linda try to comfort him? Why didn't they call me? He is not crabby at home. I'm not sure they know how to take care of my baby. Maybe something is wrong with him or with me as a parent.

Objective Comments	Parent's Thoughts
At lunchtime, Linda calls Maria to discuss Julio's fussiness. She tells her, "Julio cried when he drank his bottle this morning. I tried holding him the way you showed me, but it didn't help. Do you have any suggestions for me?" Then, when Maria picks him up at the end of the day, Linda tells her, "Julio was still a bit fussy this afternoon when he ate. I am wondering if his ears are bothering him, or if he is still just adjusting to me. What do you think?"	I wonder what's wrong. I appreciate Linda's asking me for my advice and ideas. I think that Linda is doing all she can to take care of him. Perhaps he is not used to Linda yet, but maybe he is getting sick. If this continues, I'll take him to the clinic for a checkup. I feel good about leaving Julio with Linda. I know she will call me if she has trouble with him.

Subjective Comments	Parent's Thoughts
When Matthew's father comes to pick him up at the end of the day, Mercedes tells him, "Matthew was such a good boy today. He just loves everyone."	That's a surprise. Matthew is a real challenge at home. He makes his sister cry, and he won't cooperate when we ask him to do things. If he is so good here but challenging at home, are we doing something wrong?

Objective Comments	Parent's Thoughts
When Matthew's father comes to pick him up, Mercedes tells him, "Today Matthew helped us clean up the blocks and trucks, and we only asked him one time! I handed him the basket and asked him to help put the blocks away, and he did. This afternoon, we had a volunteer in our room. Matthew sat on her lap while she read two books to him. She told us she really enjoyed him."	I have a pretty wonderful son. He is learning to clean up. I think we will encourage that at home. Also, the bedtime stories we read to him at night must be helping him listen to stories. I guess my wife was right about how important it is to read to him every day. I feel good about the way he is growing.

Communicating in More Formal Ways

In addition to informal daily exchanges, there are more formal ways to communicate with families. Some can be accomplished easily; others take more time and planning.

Daily communication form—Create a form for families to record information about their child when they arrive at the program each day. Request information that is basic to the child's daily care and explain that it helps you meet each child's current needs more effectively. You may need to encourage parents to take the time to complete this form when they bring their child. Request any information that you find necessary, such as when the child last ate, when her diaper was last changed, her general mood that day, how well she slept last night, when she will be picked up, and who will be picking her up.

Electronic mail—More and more families—and programs—have access to e-mail. Sending e-mail is an excellent way to stay in touch and to share specific information about a child.

Internet—Introduce *Teaching Strategies GOLD*™ online to families if you are using that assessment system. They can participate in a parent-to-parent message board, view their child's portfolio, and add comments or upload pictures.

Journals—Provide each family with a journal that is sent between home and school. You can each write entries to share information. While the families may or may not provide you with objective, specific, and factual information, it is essential that you do so. From time to time, you can include specific questions for families.

Newsletters—Periodically provide families with newsletters about what the children in your group have been doing. When you tell them about experiences and discoveries that the whole group has engaged in, parents can better understand their child's life at the program.

Letters to families—At the end of each of chapters 6–18, you will find a letter to families. Each sample letter describes why a particular routine or experience is an important part of the program, how you support children's learning and development, and how you hope to work together with families. Adapt the letters for your own program and send them home over a period of time—perhaps one letter a week—so that families do not feel overwhelmed with too much information. Sometimes you will want to distribute the relevant letter at a meeting during which you are talking about a routine or experience, such as how you handle hellos and good-byes.

Articles of interest, community resources, and relevant Web sites—These are resources that you can share with parents. Invite families to share the resources that they find helpful.

Notices—Written notices are a way to give every family the same information at the same time. You might want to explain a policy change, a special event, or the contagious disease of a child or staff member. Use the **mail/message boxes** for these notices.

Holding Conferences With Families

A formal conference with each family is a time to sit down together, uninterrupted, and talk as partners about caring for their child. Conferences are opportunities to share information, observations, and questions. You can solve problems together when necessary and celebrate the uniqueness of each child. If a child has a diagnosed disability, a family conference will involve the team of people who develop goals for the Individual Family Service Plan. Preparation and the many positive interactions you have already had with the family help ensure a successful conference.

When you set up conferences, involve families as much as possible.

- Arrange times that are convenient for families and find out whom they would like to include in their conferences.

- Let families know what to expect. Explain that conferences are a time to focus entirely on their children. Find out what each family's goals are for the conference. Ask what they are interested in learning about and whether there are any special issues they want to discuss.

- If language differences might be a barrier, arrange for someone to interpret. Many families know someone who can serve as an interpreter. If they do not, try to make other arrangements.

If you are using the *Teaching Strategies GOLD*™ assessment system, be sure the information you recorded in the *Child Assessment Portfolio* is complete and up-to-date. What evidence have you collected about the child's social–emotional development? Physical skills? Language development? Cognitive development? Identify the information and samples of work that will enable you to show the child's progress. Identify any areas of concern so you are prepared to discuss them with the family. This information will help you complete a "Family Conference Form" to share with each child's family. The form has places for you to summarize the child's developmental progress to date. During the conference, the rest of the form is completed together with family members. (See the Appendix of this volume.)

Start the conference by sharing your observation of something new, interesting, or delightful that their child has done or said. You may also want to ask parents questions such as "What activities do you and your child enjoy doing together now?" or "What interests your child?" Questions of this sort show your appreciation of their child and encourage families to share some of their own observations.

Next, share your summary of the child's development. Point out accomplishments and offer examples from your observation notes.

Throughout your discussion, encourage the family to share their observations, questions, challenges, and joys. Confirm that this is a time for an exchange of information and that combining what each of you knows will give both of you the clearest possible understanding of their child. In addition to recording your own ideas, ask the family for their ideas when you discuss the other sections of the form. Family conferences are also good times to update the "Individual Care Plan" form you have for each child.

Talk together about expectations for the child's development and complete the "Next Steps" section of the "Family Conference Form" with the child's family. This will become your blueprint for working with the child during the next 3 months or so until the next assessment checkpoint and conference. Keep it where you will have ready access to it, so you can remind yourself of areas you want to focus on during the next few months. At the next conference, the form can serve as a starting point for your discussion.

Making Home Visits

Home visits are another way of communicating with families. They provide a unique opportunity to see a child and family in their most comfortable setting. Some programs require home visits, but others do not. In either case, families should be given some choice about whether they want a home visit. When a home visit is too stressful for a family, it will not achieve its purpose.

Talk with families about the purpose of the visit. Let them know ahead of time why you are coming. Arrange a time that is convenient for both of you. Families may be anxious or excited about your visit. Reassure them and help them feel comfortable about your presence in their homes.

When you make home visits, follow your program's established policies and procedures. Here are some general guidelines to keep in mind.

- Decide ahead of time what you want to accomplish. Is it simply to introduce yourself and meet the family or do you have additional goals?
- Ask the family about their goals for the visit. Address as many of their requests as possible.
- Review the enrollment materials before going on the visit, so that you are familiar with the names of family members and information about the family.
- Develop and use a home visiting plan to help you prepare for the visit.
- Contact the family to set up a good time for the visit. Agree on a date and time and give them an idea of how long you will be staying.
- Get directions to the home. If you feel unsafe going alone, take a colleague from the program with you or arrange for the family to visit you at the program.
- Gather the materials and information you will need before making the visit.
- After the visit, record any information or observations that you want to remember.

These approaches to communicating with families will help you obtain the full benefits of a true partnership. You will have the information you need to care for the child, families will gain confidence in you, and children will be more likely to thrive in your care.

Involving Families in the Program

Most families want and need to be involved in their child's life at the program. For some, this is the first time they have left their child in the care of someone other than a family member. For infants, toddlers, and twos, their families' presence at the program is the best way to help them experience the connection between their home and your program.

Offering a Variety of Ways to Be Involved

While some families are able to arrange their work schedules to feed or eat lunch with their children, join the group for a neighborhood walk, or assist in the room for a morning, many are not able to participate in these ways. They may feel lucky if they have a few extra minutes to spend when dropping off and picking up their children. Offer a variety of options that match families' interests, skills, schedules, and other responsibilities so that family members feel welcome and competent when they come. During the enrollment process, ask families how they would like to participate.

Families are more likely to participate if you let them know how much you value their involvement and how much it benefits their child and the program. A grandmother who comes to hold her grandson and who reads and talks with him and another baby will see how much her help is appreciated. She may even offer to come regularly. However, the parent who sews two covers for the bouncing mattress might never see the children use them. Be sure to thank her and explain the advantage of having two covers: "Bouncing is one of the children's favorite activities. Now we can wash one while the other is in use." Show her some photographs of the children using a new cover. Similarly, acknowledge the parent who produces the newsletter by listing his name in every issue.

There are many ways for families to be involved in the program. Consider some of the following suggestions.

Jobs—On index cards, list program-related needs that families can fill at home. Jobs could include repairing broken toys, shopping at yard sales for water toys such as measuring cups and spoons, and making books or other materials for the room.

Projects—At an evening or weekend session, families can work together to improve the program by such things as painting walls, making a new sandbox, or preparing a garden plot. Some projects can be completed by families at their convenience over a period of time. Celebrate when a project is completed.

Useful junk—Every home has disposable items that the program can recycle as play materials. Empty food containers, ribbons, wrapping paper, and paper towel tubes are among the items that a program can use. Try asking for one or two specific items at a time.

Book reviews—Invite families to read and review children's books or books on child development and parenting. Provide a book review form to record the title, author, publisher, price, and comments. For children's books, leave space on the form for the family to record the ages for which the book is appropriate, what the book is about, and why they and their child liked it. Use these recommendations to select books for the children. Families can also review music CDs and tapes.

Family dinner night—Plan an event that encourages families eat dinner together before going home. Dinner might be a meal planned and prepared with the older children or something simpler, such as pizza.

Family playtime—Open the center for an evening or a weekend afternoon so that families can come with their children and participate in program experiences together.

A room for families—If space is available, consider creating a resource area for families. Include comfortable places to sit, resources of interest to families, and, if possible, computers with Internet access. Some programs find that family involvement increases dramatically when families are invited to use the washer and dryer that are reserved for them.

Class photo album—Provide an album and ask a volunteer to insert photographs you have collected of the children in your group. Display the photo album prominently and include a cover page thanking the person who made it. Include it in the family lending-library.

Participating in the Program

When families are encouraged to spend time at the program, they see how you interact with their children and learn new ideas to try at home. You gain extra help, and their presence shows children that their homes and the program are connected.

Keep in mind that a setting for infants, toddlers, and twos can be an intimidating place for some family members. They may be unsure of what you expect and what they should be doing. Sometimes children behave differently when family members, especially their parents, visit the program. They may act out or insist on their parent's full attention. It is important to prepare parents for these possibilities and to assure them that such behavior is to be expected. Advise them to pay special attention to their child, even as they interact with other children.

Here are some suggestions for making participation a positive experience for families.

Speak personally with each family member. Greet families when they arrive. Offer a quick update about their child and what you have planned for the period of time they will be with you.

Explain the procedures you want them to follow. If a family member will be helping out with routines such as handwashing and feeding, explain the procedures you follow to keep children healthy. If possible, post charts illustrating the steps so you do not have to explain them each time. If the family member is helping in an infant room, be sure to have enough shoe covers available. Shoe covers help keep the floor clean for the infants who spend some of their waking hours on it.

Provide guidance clearly and respectfully. You are responsible for the program environment, and you have an overall sense of what is needed to keep things running smoothly. If two parents who came for lunch are standing in the corner talking with each other while their children are seeking their attention, you might say, "Your children are so excited to see you here, it's hard for them to wait to show you what they are doing. Why don't you join them until we are ready for lunch?"

Offer concrete suggestions about what to do. Plan activities that family members can enjoy with children. "I'm going to bring out some new balls. I think the children will enjoy rolling them back and forth with you." Invite their help when you need it. "We're getting ready to go outside in a few minutes. We could really use your help with putting the children's jackets on."

Avoid lengthy conversations. Explain that lengthy conversations must be postponed until a time when you are not directly responsible for the children. "Let's set up a meeting to talk about this later. Right now I need to be with the children, and I want to be able to give you my full attention when we talk."

Make the physical environment manageable. Labeling shelves and drawers will help families find the supplies they need without having to ask you. If possible, take families on a short tour of the room to explain what goes on in each area.

Share information about how children develop and learn. Display the curricular objectives and explain how children are developing and what they are learning at the program.

When family members participate in the program, the steps you have taken to make it a positive experience will make them more likely to want to continue.

Sharing Information and Parenting Tips

Families often look to you for advice and information. Discussing aspects of the curriculum and sharing related resources with families can really help them understand the value of the experiences you provide in the program and how to support their children's development and learning at home effectively. Several resources enable you to provide information to families.

1. At the end of each chapter of *The Creative Curriculum® for Infants, Toddlers & Twos, Volume 2* you will find a sample letter titled "Sharing Thoughts About…" Each of the five letters about routines describes how you support children's learning during the program and ways families can work with you to make the routine run smoothly. The letters about play experiences explain what happens in the program and suggest ways for families to provide similar experiences at home. You may want to share the letters about routines as you develop each child's individual care plan with his or her family. The letters about experiences might be shared when a child seems to be developing an interest in playing with particular materials.

2. *Our Program for Infants, Toddlers & Twos* is a small booklet from Teaching Strategies that describes all aspects of a program that implements *The Creative Curriculum®*. It helps families learn more about what you do and why, and how they can engage their children in rich learning experiences at home. This booklet might be given to each family when their child enters the program, or it can be given to families at a workshop or during family conferences.

3. Another valuable resource to offer families is a set of activities called *The Creative Curriculum® LearningGames®*. These activities were originally developed for the Abecedarian Project, which is one of the most frequently referenced projects that worked with families of children birth to age 5 and that produced long-lasting, positive results. Some of the long-term benefits for the children were improved performance in math and reading, a reduction in grade retention, and increased college attendance.

4. The first three books of *LearningGames®* activities are for children under age 3. One is for children aged birth–12 months, another is for children aged 12–24 months, and one is for children aged 24–36 months. Each book includes directions for a series of games that are arranged in approximate order of increasing difficulty, a checklist to track which games you give to each family, and an overview of development for that year of life. Each game is presented on the front and back of a full page, which is perforated so it can be removed easily and given to a family. An engaging photograph shows an adult playing the game with one or more children. The brief text on the front page describes the main idea and how the game supports children's development.

The back of each page has four sections:

- "Why this is important" explains how the activity supports a child's current and future development and learning. It tells the benefits of playing the game.
- "What you do" gives step-by-step instructions for playing the game. They include examples of what a family member might say to and ask a child as they play the game together as well as other ways to respond to the child.
- "Ready to move on?" and "Another idea" present a slightly more challenging variation of the game to try after the child has mastered the original version.
- The last section suggests a children's book related to the topic of the game.

Programs that can provide these resources for families will need one *LearningGames* book for each child and a system for keeping track of which games have been sent home for each family. *Using The Creative Curriculum® LearningGames With Families* helps you use *LearningGames®* to support your work with children and their families. For home visitors who regularly work with families, *A Home Visitor's Guide to The Creative Curriculum® Learning Games®* explains how to use *LearningGames®* in home settings. (See TeachingStrategies.com for more information.)

Responding to Challenging Situations

Despite all of the positive steps you take to build a partnership with each family, you will encounter challenging situations. Even in the best relationships, you will find that misunderstandings and conflicts emerge. Some families are struggling with meeting basic needs, and the ongoing stress makes it difficult for them to be available to their children. You may also have children with disabilities in your program, and their families require special understanding and support. Challenging situations must be handled carefully and positively in order to maintain a partnership with every family.

Resolving Differences: A Partnership Approach

If you work with families who share your values and beliefs and have similar life experiences and personal characteristics, you are more likely to interpret what they say and do in the same way as they do. If you work with families who are very different from you—and if you know little about their beliefs and practices—miscommunication and misunderstandings can easily take place. Understanding and respecting practices that are different from your own help you build positive relationships with all families.

When the adults in their lives share a consistent approach, children gain a sense of continuity that helps them feel safe and secure in child care. This does not mean that you have to agree about everything. There will probably be times when you and a family have different points of view about caring for their child. The question is this: "How can we work out our differences in a positive way?"

Here are examples of how misunderstandings can occur because your views about a situation differ from that of a family member. Following each example, a resolution that respects the partnership is suggested.

Situation	Your View	The Family's View
After careful observations over time, you are concerned that a toddler's language is delayed. You suggest an evaluation by a speech specialist. The parents fail to make an appointment with a specialist.	If a problem exists, it should be identified as early as possible. Parents should want to get all the help they can get for their child.	My child is fine. There's nothing wrong.

For a number of reasons, parents might resist a recommendation to have their child evaluated by a specialist. It is not unusual for parents to deny that there might be a problem. (See the section of this chapter on "Supporting the Families of Children With Disabilities.") If you suspect that this is the reason for their reluctance, provide information, suggest that all of you observe the child more carefully for a few weeks, and keep in touch about what you learn. It is also possible that the family lacks transportation to get to a specialist, or they might be uneasy about managing an unfamiliar system of services. You might offer to have someone from the program go along or arrange to have the specialist observe the child at the program.

Situation	Your View	The Family's View
The mother of a toddler unzips her daughter's coat and hangs it in her cubby near her mittens and boots. Knowing that this child is able to do that herself, you say, "Keisha, you know how to unzip and hang up your coat. Tomorrow, show your Mommy how you can do things for yourself."	Developing personal care skills and developing independence are important objectives for children. I don't want to have to do everything for every child. Keisha's mother is treating her like a baby.	Helping my child is one way I show her how much her family loves her. I want to care for her, especially just before I have to say good-bye for the day. There's plenty of time for her to learn to take care of herself.

You might want to encourage children to do as much for themselves as possible, but some families do things for their children as a sign of love even when the children can do them independently. With this understanding, you can support a mother's practice of unzipping, removing, and hanging up her child's coat. At the same time, you might share with the parent that, when she is not available, her child is learning to care for herself, which is an important life skill. Explain how helpful this is to you because you are responsible for a whole group of children.

Situation	Your View	The Family's View
A family requests that you continue their practice at home of toilet training their 12-month-old child. They explain how they are aware of when their child has to urinate and defecate and that they manage to take him to the potty in time.	"Catching" a child in time to bring him to the potty is not toilet learning. Children let us know when they have the muscle control and awareness to use the toilet. That is the most appropriate time to begin the process of toilet learning.	It is important for us to train our children to use the toilet at this age. We did it with our other children, and it works just fine.

Toilet learning is a topic about which you and families are likely to have strong feelings and perhaps different approaches. It is helpful to discuss the family's approach to toilet learning when they are first considering enrolling their child in your program. You should also explain the program's philosophy and the steps that you typically use when helping children learn to use the toilet. This may prevent some problems before they arise.

When toileting practices differ, it is important to listen to the family's perspective and find some aspect of their approach to affirm. "As you can imagine, it's more challenging with a group of children. I think there is something we can do, however. We check every child's diaper regularly each hour. We could take your child to the toilet at that time and see how that works." This approach conveys your appreciation of the family's preference without making a commitment that you might not be able to honor.

Situation	Your View	The Family's View
When you first meet the grandfather of a toddler, he tells you that he doesn't understand why you do not spank his grandson for hitting other children.	You teach children to be gentle with others by modeling gentleness and guiding their behavior in positive ways. You stop children when they hit others and show them how to verbalize their thoughts and feelings instead of hitting.	The grandfather believes in using a strong-hand approach to raising children. His philosophy is "Spare the rod, spoil the child." It worked for him with his children. He is concerned about his grandson's behavior.

When a family member you do not know well comes to discuss a concern, it is helpful to begin by taking a few minutes to get to know the person better before attempting to address the issue. Explain that you understand his concerns: "It sounds like it's very important to you that your grandson learn to behave well. Is that right?" Then take the time to discuss your program's approach to promoting positive behavior. Share the social–emotional objectives and the progressions for developing self-control and prosocial behaviors. Then explain how you support children's learning.

Working Through Conflicts

If you do not try to resolve an issue that is bothering you, you will probably become annoyed. The children will sense that something is not quite right. Avoiding an issue rarely solves the problem and sometimes makes it worse. It is worth making the effort to find a resolution.

> **Matthew** (22 months) has been at the center for just one month, but each week his parents come later and later to pick him up. The program closes at 6:00 p.m., and Grace needs to leave on time to attend a class. She is becoming annoyed with Matthew's parents because her reminders have not made a difference. Finally, she arranges a conference to explain to them how difficult it is for her when they are late. Matthew's father says they did not know they were causing a problem. If they know they will be late from now on, Matthew's parents will have a cousin pick him up.

When a family member is clearly upset about a problem, you want to respond in ways that lead to a positive resolution. It is helpful to know what steps to follow to resolve the conflict. Because conversations about children can sometimes be emotional, they are better handled away from the children and other families. If you are working with children when an upset family member approaches you, suggest delaying the conversation until you can find someone to take over. Then you can give the family member your full attention in a more private place.

The steps of conflict resolution are explained on the next few pages. Examples of how they can be applied are also given.

Remain calm and help others to remain calm. When emotions are strong, the first step is to defuse the situation. A good way to remain calm and help others remain calm is to seek to understand the family member's position and validate their feelings. By asking open-ended questions, you can gather details that enable you to understand the significance of what is being said. This approach helps reduce any defensiveness that you and the parent might be feeling. When feelings have been defused, conversations are more likely to be rational. To be sure that you have heard and understood correctly, restate what you think you heard them say. This also lets them know that you are listening.

What a Parent Says	How You Respond
"I'm very upset, so I need to talk to you right now. My son Jerome is afraid to come here, and it's all because of another child in your group."	"You do sound upset. Let me call someone to take my place for a few minutes. Then we can talk where it is quiet." After the director comes to take over, you find a quiet room to meet with Jerome's mother and say, "I'd like to have a better understanding of the problem. What seems to be troubling Jerome?"
"Jerome is afraid of that new child. I think his name is Steven. He says that Steven hits other children and that he has hit Jerome. I want you to keep my child away from this bully."	"You are telling me that you don't care for the way that Steven behaves around other children. You want us to keep him away from your child. Is that correct?"
"Yes, that is what I am saying."	"That is a problem. We certainly don't want Jerome or any child to feel unsafe here."

Clarify the problem and agree on goals. In order to come to an agreement *together,* the problem needs to be clarified and discussed. It is important to allow family members to explain their perspective and for you to share your program policies regarding the issue. Be careful not to attempt to solve the problem too quickly, yourself, without asking for the family members' ideas. Without negating their request or getting into a discussion about another child, talk about your shared vision for all children. You might also find it helpful to share the specific objectives from *Objectives for Development & Learning* that relate to the issue and discuss the examples. Describe the way your program supports children in acquiring the skills that are related to the issue being discussed.

What a Parent Says	How You Respond
"How can Jerome feel safe here when he is worried about Steven's hitting him? He's starting to have nightmares, and I know it's because he is afraid. What will you do to keep Steven away from my child?"	"We both want Jerome to know he is safe here. I can assure you that one of our goals is to teach all of the children to express their feelings in acceptable ways, without hitting others."
"Well, it doesn't seem like you are doing a very good job with Steven. He only knows how to hit."	"Let me share the goals and objectives of our curriculum with you. Here are the objectives for helping children learn about themselves and others. You can see the steps that children take in relation to each objective. This is how we know what support and guidance each child needs to learn to relate positively to others."
"How do you guide them?"	"One of the ways is by modeling what we want the children to do, how we want them to relate to each other. We also talk with the children when they hurt other children."
"That's all well and good, but, while you are teaching the children to relate positively, my child is still afraid."	"I respect your request to keep Jerome safe. What I hear you saying is that you want us to keep the children apart. Am I right?"
"Well, yes, it is. That's the only way I'll know my child is safe and comfortable here."	"We want you and your child to know that this is a safe place. We can certainly agree on that goal."

Together, generate solutions. Once feelings have been calmed, the problem clarified, and there is some agreement about goals, you will want to resolve the problem in a way that satisfies both you and the family. One way to start finding a solution is to ask for their ideas. You may have an idea of how to solve the problem, but your goal is to involve the family in the problem-solving process. By being willing to share control in the process, you send messages that the family's opinion and ideas count and that you are *partners* in caring for their child.

What a Parent Says	How You Respond
"So what are you going to do?"	"As you can imagine, keeping children apart is hard. Toddlers move around a lot and are free to choose where they want to play. What can we do to help Jerome feel safe?"
"I am not sure. I think that Jerome needs to know you will be watching out for him."	"My co-teacher and I plan to stay close to Jerome and Steven whenever they are playing near each other. Will that help Jerome feel safe?"
"Yes, that would help."	"We will also focus on helping all of the children relate positively to each other. I can give you an update each day. What if we try this for a week and make a point of talking again?"
"All right."	"Good. We'll try this for a week and see whether our plan makes a difference."

Continue the dialogue. Once a possible solution is identified, plan to check with each other to discuss whether it is working for you and the family. If the solution is not working well, you will want to talk with the family again and come up with another solution. Reassure them that you will continue to look for solutions with them until the problem is resolved. Use *Objectives for Development & Learning* to help you and the family better understand children's abilities and needs, and to identify what all of you can do to continue to support the child.

What a Parent Says	How You Respond
"I think Jerome is feeling better now. He's not so afraid any more."	"That's wonderful news. Why do you think that is?"
"For one thing, we've been talking with him at home, reassuring him that his teachers will keep him safe. I've also been telling him that, if anyone hits him, he should tell them to stop!"	"I'm sure that what you are doing at home has helped. We have seen a lot of progress here since we began emphasizing positive ways of playing together. Your concern really helped everyone."
"That's good to know. I was a little afraid to bring it up at first, but I'm glad I did."	"I hope you will always feel free to bring up any concerns. It's the only way we can resolve them. After all, this is a partnership."

Conflicts are a normal part of sharing the care of a young child. Recognizing this fact helps you to think about conflicts as opportunities to understand a family's point of view and find ways to partner with the family. The more you know about children and families, the better you will be able to determine the best approach to handling conflicts.

Supporting Families Who Are Under Stress

Families experience different kinds of stress, and they may have difficulty coping. Ongoing and unrelenting stress can come from many sources. Here are just a few examples:

- living in a violent community
- seeking employment or job training without knowing whether they will be able to continue bringing their child to the program
- long commutes to a job
- a job that does not allow flexibility in work hours to accommodate family needs
- a family member with a physical disability, chronic illness, cognitive delays, low literacy skills, or mental illness
- domestic and/or substance abuse
- adapting to a new culture and/or language
- substandard, overcrowded housing or living in a shelter
- barriers to health care

Parents who are under stress from these or other situations do not always have the emotional energy or physical resources to nurture their children. Sometimes they cannot meet their children's most basic needs. They may not be able to solve problems, communicate with their children, or give them the attention and affirmation they need. Their discipline may be inconsistent, overly punitive, or nonexistent. For many children in these circumstances, life is unpredictable and dangerous, and their confusion may manifest itself in anger, withdrawal, or fearfulness in your program.

While you are not expected to try to solve a family's problems, you can take steps to help when you notice that a family is under stress. Recognize that everyone handles stress differently and that you should not make assumptions about how a family member is coping. Be as supportive as you can. Avoid adding to the stress by being overly critical, such as when a parent forgets to bring boots for her child despite several reminders. Also be mindful of parental stress when you need to discuss a problem you are having with their child. Sometimes it is wise to wait for a better time. Seek ways to affirm the family member.

Your program might have social services and family support workers who can conduct a family assessment to learn about a family's situation and then help find the resources they need. At a minimum, every program can put together information for families, including

- an up-to-date list of community agencies and hotlines for referrals
- brochures and resources for families to borrow
- a list of support groups that deal with family issues

Parenting is one of the most important jobs in the world, yet there is very little training for this critical role. Adults who were fortunate enough to have caring, nurturing experiences when they were children have a solid foundation for becoming supportive parents. Those who had less constructive experiences still want the best for their children and are doing what they think is needed. Although some parents do things that distress you, hold to the belief that most are doing the best they can. Learn as much as you can about the strengths and needs of each family so that you have realistic expectations and can individualize your approach to your partnership. Your way of working with one family will not necessarily be the same as with another.

Supporting the Families of Children With Disabilities

It is very possible that some of the children in your program will have special needs. Many of these children and families will already be receiving early intervention services for a diagnosed disability. Others may have special needs that have not yet been identified. Your factual observations and *Objectives for Development & Learning* can play a role in helping the family and specialists identify the child's special needs and obtain the needed services.

When parents realize that their child is not developing typically, they often experience a mix of emotions that is unique to dealing with this new reality. Knowing the emotional stages experienced by many families of children with disabilities will help you offer appropriate support.[27]

1. **Denial**—Initially parents may deny the child's special needs or disability. Recognize that this is a first step in coming to terms with their child's disability and do not put any pressure on the family to accept what may be obvious to others.

2. **Projection of blame**—A common reaction to learning that their child is not perfect is for families to want to blame someone else. There may or may not be any basis for the accusations some families make. You might hear family members say things such as, "If only they would have…." You may even become a target of blame. Again, patience and a willingness to listen without taking sides will help you and the family through this stage.

3. **Fear**—At this stage, the family is still learning about the special needs of their child. The information is probably new to them, and they may question it. You or someone in your program can offer support by helping them sort through the information and by learning about the disability, yourself.

4. **Guilt**—Some families worry that they did not do all they should have to prevent the disability. Their thinking might or might not be rational. Remember that this is a difficult time for the family. At this stage, the family may find it helpful if you offer ideas about channeling their energy into activities to support their child.

5. **Mourning or grief**—The reality of a disability often brings tremendous grief, pain, and disappointment. Families must work through many emotions before being able to accept their child's disability. You can help by listening and showing that you care.

6. **Withdrawal**—Withdrawing in order to manage their powerful emotions is often a healthy and essential step for families. You may become concerned about family members as you see them withdraw and become isolated. Continue to communicate with them, and offer your understanding and respect for what they are experiencing.

7. **Rejection**—At this stage, the family member may show some signs of rejecting their child's disability. This can mean failing to recognize the child's capabilities and strengths or setting unrealistic goals for the child. The objectives for development and learning and your factual observation notes can help the family member realize their child's strengths and capabilities and set realistic goals for the child.

8. **Acceptance**—At this stage, the parent is able to accept the child with his disability and offer the support that helps him develop and learn.

Recognize that there is no set timetable for how quickly or slowly family members progress through these stages. Not all families go through each stage, and sometimes family members cycle through the stages more than once. An event, such as seeing another child who is developing at a typical pace, can trigger feelings all over again. It may be painful for you to observe families while they are experiencing the powerful emotions involved during these stages.

It is important to recognize the limits of your own time, energy, knowledge, and skills with regard to a child's disability and the family's needs. You can encourage family members to seek additional support from specialists who are more familiar with their child's disability than you are. A list of available resources may be helpful, but they will probably need the assistance of a social worker or someone who knows how to negotiate the maze of special services. This person should be someone who can guide them through the process of getting help and support for themselves and their child.

Conclusion

When you achieve partnerships with children's families, everyone benefits. Children feel more secure and comfortable when their families and teachers share their knowledge respectfully and interact positively. Children are more likely to experience consistency in the care they receive when families are invited to share what they know and what they want for their child. Families feel more secure when they leave their child in the care of someone who makes the effort to build a relationship with them. When you share your knowledge of child development in a way that helps families understand the importance of what their very young children are able to do, families gain confidence in their parenting. You gain the families' valuable insights about their children, and that enables you to provide more individualized care. As partners in the care of their child, families are more likely to feel as though they are an important part of your program and to offer their support.

Appendix

Individual Care Plan—Family Information Form
Individual Care Plan
Child Planning Form
Group Planning Form
Family Conference Form

Note: These forms are also available from
www.TeachingStrategies.com/it2-forms

Individual Care Plan
Family Information Form

Child:	
Child's Date of Birth:	
Teacher:	
Family Member(s):	
Date:	

Arrival

What time will you usually arrive at the center? _____

What will help you and your child say good-bye to each other in the morning?

Diapering and Toileting

What type of diapers do you use? _____

How often do you change your child's diaper? When does your child usually need a diaper change?

Are there any special instructions for diaper changes?

Is your child beginning to use the toilet? If so, are there any special instructions for toileting?

Sleeping

How will we know that your child is tired and needs to sleep?

When does your child usually sleep? For how long does he or she usually sleep?

What helps your child to fall asleep?

We put babies to sleep on their backs. Is your baby used to sleeping on his or her back? **Y / N**

How does your child wake up? Does he or she wake up quickly or slowly? Does your child like to be taken out of the crib immediately or to lie alone in the crib for a few minutes before being held?

Individual Care Plan
Family Information Form, continued

Eating

Babies:

Are you breast-feeding or bottle-feeding your baby? _____

If breast-feeding, will you come to the center to breast-feed? **Y / N**

    If so, at what time? _____

    If not, will you send expressed breast milk? _____

If bottle-feeding,

    What kind of formula do you use? _____

    How do you prepare the bottles? _____

    How much do you prepare at one time? _____

    How much does your baby drink at one time? _____

Does your baby drink bottles of water during the day? **Y / N**

    If so, when and how much? _____

Is your baby eating solid foods? **Y / N**

    If so, which ones? _____

    When? _____

    How do you prepare your baby's solid foods? _____

    How much does your baby eat at one time? _____

How is your baby used to being fed (in what position)? _____

Does your baby eat any finger foods? If so, which ones? _____

All Children:

What are some of your child's favorite foods? _____

What foods does your child dislike? _____

Is your child sensitive or allergic to any foods? If so, please list them.

Are there any foods that you don't want your child to eat?

The Creative Curriculum® for Infants, Toddlers & Twos

Individual Care Plan
Family Information Form, continued

Dressing

Is there anything special that we should know about dressing and undressing your child?

Awake Time

How does your baby like to be held? What position does your baby prefer when awake?

In what language do you speak and sing with your child at home?

What language does your child use when talking and singing with family members?

What does your child like to do when awake?

How do you play with your child?

Departure

What time will you usually come to pick up your child?

What will help you and your child say hello to each other at the end of the day?

Individual Care Plan

Child:
Child's Date of Birth:
Teacher:
Family Member(s):
Date:

Arrival	**Eating**
Diapering	**Dressing**
Sleeping	**Departure**

©2011 Teaching Strategies, Inc., P.O. Box 42243, Washington, DC 20015; www.TeachingStrategies.com
Permission is granted to duplicate the material on this page for use in programs implementing *The Creative Curriculum® for Infants, Toddlers & Twos*.

Child Planning Form

Teacher(s):
Group:
Week of:

Child:
Current information:

Plans:

Child:
Current information:

Plans:

Child:
Current information:

Plans:

Child:
Current information:

Plans:

Child:
Current information:

Plans:

Child:
Current information:

Plans:

Current information includes new accomplishments, interests, dislikes, family news, and special needs.

©2011 Teaching Strategies, Inc., P.O. Box 42243, Washington, DC 20015; www.TeachingStrategies.com
Permission is granted to duplicate the material on this page for use in programs implementing *The Creative Curriculum® for Infants, Toddlers & Twos.*

Group Planning Form

| Teacher(s): |
| Group: |
| Week of: |

Changes to the Environment:

Changes to Routines and Schedule:

Family Involvement:

	Special Experiences I Plan to Offer This Week				
	Monday	**Tuesday**	**Wednesday**	**Thursday**	**Friday**
Indoor Experiences					
Outdoor Experiences					

Thoughts for Next Week:

Family Conference Form

Child's Name: _____ Date: _____

Teacher(s): _____ Family Members(s): _____

Summary of Development & Learning
Partner with a family member(s) to complete this form.

Describe this child's strengths in social–emotional, physical, language, and cognitive development:
Describe this child's strengths in learning literacy, math, science and technology, social studies, and the arts:
Plan for this child's development and learning:

Teacher(s) Signature(s): _____ Family Member(s) Signature (s): _____

©2011 Teaching Strategies, Inc., P.O. Box 42243, Washington, DC 20015; www.TeachingStrategies.com
Permission is granted to duplicate the material on this page for use in programs implementing *The Creative Curriculum® for Infants, Toddlers & Twos.*

References

[1] National Association for the Education of Young Children. (1997). *Developmentally appropriate practice in early childhood programs serving children from birth through age 8: A position statement of the National Association for the Education of Young Children.* Retrieved June 28, 2006, from http://www.naeyc.org/about/positions/pdf/PSDAP98.PDF

[2] Maslow, A. H. (1999). *Toward a psychology of being* (3rd ed.). New York, NY: J. Wiley & Sons.

[3] Brazelton, T. B., & Greenspan, S. (2000). *The irreducible needs of children: What every child must have to grow, learn, and flourish.* Cambridge, MA: Da Capo Press.

[4] Erikson, E. (1993). *Childhood and society.* New York, NY: W. W. Norton & Company, Inc.

[5] Greenspan, S. (1999). *Building healthy minds: The six experiences that create intelligence and emotional growth in babies and young children.* New York, NY: Perseus Publishing.

[6] Bowlby, J. (1969). *Attachment and loss: Vol. 1. Attachment.* New York: Basic Books.

[7] Ainsworth, M., Blehar, M., Waters, E., & Wall, S. (1978). *Patterns of attachment.* Hillsdale, NJ: Erlbaum.

[8] Masten, A. S. (2001). Ordinary magic: Resilience processes in development. *American Psychologist, 56,* 227–238.

Benard, B. (2004). *Resiliency: What we have learned.* San Francisco, CA: WestEd.

[9] Piaget, J., & Inhelder, B. (2000). *The psychology of the child* (H. Weaver, Trans.). New York, NY: Basic Books.

[10] Vygotsky, L. S. (1999). The collected works of L. S. Vygotsky: Scientific legacy (M. J. Hall, Trans.). In R. W. Rieber, Ed., *Cognition and language: A series in psycholinguistics* (Vol. 6). London: Kluwer Academic/Plenum Publishers.

[11] Shonkoff, J. P., & Phillips, D. A. (Eds.). (2000). *From neurons to neighborhoods: The science of early childhood development.* Washington, DC: National Academy Press.

[12] Ibid.

[13] Ibid.

[14] Cole, M., Cole, S. R., & Lightfoot, C. (2005). *The development of children* (5th ed.). New York, NY: Worth Publishers.

[15] From *Temperament: Theory and Practice*, by S. Chess & A. Thomas, 1996, New York, NY: Brunner/Mazel, Inc. Copyright 1996 by Brunner/Mazel, Inc. Adapted with permission of Routledge/Taylor & Francis Group, LLC.

[16] Genesee, F. *Bilingual acquisition.* Retrieved March 21, 2002, from http://www.earlychildhood.com/Articles/index.cfm?FuseAction=Article&A=38

Snow, C. E. (1997, November 1). The myths around being bilingual. *NABE News, 29,* 36.

References

[17] American Academy of Pediatrics & American Public Health Association. (2002). *Caring for our children: National health and safety performance standards: Guidelines for out-of-home care programs: A joint collaborative project of American Academy of Pediatrics, American Public Health Association, and National Resource Center for Health and Safety in Child Care* (2nd ed.). Elk Grove Village, IL: The Academy.

[18] From *Heart Start: The Emotional Foundations of School Readiness* (p. 7), by ZERO TO THREE, 1992, Washington, DC: Author. Copyright 1992 by the author. Retrieved February 7, 2006, from http://www.zerotothree.org/sch_read.html Adapted with permission.

[19] Hart, B., & Risley, T. R. (1995). *Meaningful differences in the everyday experience of young American children.* Baltimore, MD: Brookes Publishing.

[20] Hart, B., & Risley, T. R. (1995). *Meaningful differences in the everyday experience of young American children.* Baltimore, MD: Brookes Publishing.

Snow, C. E., Burns, M. S., & Griffin, P. (Eds.). (1998). *Preventing reading difficulties in young children.* Washington, DC: National Academy Press.

[21] Weitzman, E., & Greenberg, J. (2002). *Learning language and loving it* (2nd ed., pp. 37–49). Toronto: The Hanen Centre.

[22] Schickedanz, J. (1999). *Much more than the ABCs: The early stages of reading and writing.* Washington, DC: National Association for the Education of Young Children.

[23] Geist, E. (2004). Infants and toddlers exploring mathematics. In D. Koralek, Ed., *Spotlight on young children and math*, Washington, DC: National Association for the Education of Young Children.

[24] National Council of Teachers of Mathematics. (2000). *Principles and standards for school mathematics.* Reston, VA: Author.

[25] National Association for the Education of Young Children. (2005). Teacher-child ratios within group size. *NAEYC early childhood program standards and accreditation performance criteria.* Retrieved June 14, 2006, from http://www.naeyc.org/accreditation/performance_criteria/teacher_child_ratios.html

[26] Greenman, J., & Stonehouse, A. W. (1994, September). Reality bites: Biting at the center—Part 1. *Exchange.*

National Association for the Education of Young Children. (1996). Biters: Why they do it and what to do about it. *Early Years Are Learning Years.* Retrieved June 22, 2006, from http://www.naeyc.org/ece/1996/08.asp

[27] From *Parents as Partners in Education: Families and Schools Working Together* (6th ed.), by E. H. Berger, 2004, Upper Saddle River, NJ: Pearson Education. Copyright 2004 by Pearson Education. Adapted with permission.

General Resources

Baker, A., & Manfredi-Petitt, L. (2004). *Relationships, the heart of quality care: Creating community among adults in early care settings.* Washington, DC: National Association for the Education of Young Children.

Bardige, B. (2005). *At a loss for words: How America is failing our children and what we can do about it.* Philadelphia, PA: Temple University Press.

Bardige, B., & Segal, M. (2005). *Building literacy with love: A guide for teachers and caregivers of children birth through age 5,* Washington, DC: ZERO TO THREE Press.

Berk, L. (2004). *Infants and children: Prenatal through middle childhood.* Needham Heights, MA: Allyn & Bacon.

Brazelton, T. B. (1992). *Touchpoints birth to three: The essential reference for the early years.* Cambridge, MA: Da Capo Press.

Brilliant Beginnings, LLC. (1999). *Baby brain basics guidebook: Birth to 12 months.* Long Beach, CA: Author.

Carlson, V., Feng, X., & Harwood, R. (2004). The "ideal baby": A look at the intersection of temperament and culture. *Zero to Three, 24*(4), 22–28.

Day, M., & Parlakian, R. (2004). *How culture shapes social-emotional development: Implications for practice in infant-family programs.* Washington, DC: ZERO TO THREE Press.

Egeland, B., & Erickson, M. (1999). *Attachment theory and research.* Retrieved June 30, 2005, from http://www.zerotothree.org/vol20-2.html

Ezell, H. K., & Justice, L. M. (2005). *Shared storybook reading: Building young children's language and emergent literacy skills.* Baltimore, Maryland: Paul H. Brookes Publishing Co.

Gonzalez-Mena, J. (2005). *Diversity in early care and education: Honoring differences.* New York, NY: McGraw-Hill.

Greenman, J. (2005). *Caring spaces, learning places: Children's environments that work.* Redmond, WA: Exchange Press, Inc.

Greenman, J., & Stonehouse, A. (1996). *Prime times: A handbook for excellence in infant and toddler programs.* St. Paul, MN: Redleaf Press.

Grotberg, E. (1995). *A guide to promoting resilience in children: Strengthening the human spirit.* Retrieved June 30, 2005, from http://resilnet.uiuc.edu/library/grotb95b.html

Hart, B., & Risley, T. R. (1999). *The social world of children learning to talk.* Baltimore, MD: Paul H. Brookes Publishing Co., Inc.

Honig, A. (2002). *Secure relationships: Nurturing infant/toddler attachment in early care settings.* Washington, DC: National Association for the Education of Young Children.

General Resources

Howes, C. & Ritchie, S. (2002). *A matter of trust: Connecting teachers and learners in the early childhood classroom.* New York, NY: Teachers College Press.

Jalongo, M. R. (2004). *Young children and picture books.* Washington, DC: National Association for the Education of Young Children.

Kohl, M. F. (2002). *First art: Art experiences for toddlers and twos.* Beltsville, MD: Gryphon House, Inc.

Lally, J. R., Griffin, A., Fenichel, E., Segal, M., Szanton, E., & Weissbourd, B. (2003). *Caring for infants and toddlers in groups: Developmentally appropriate practice.* Washington, DC: ZERO TO THREE Press.

Lally, J. R., & Mangione, P. (2006, July). The uniqueness of infancy demands a responsive approach to care. *Young Children, 61*(4), 14–20.

Lerner, C., & Dombro, A. (2000). *Learning and growing together: Understanding and supporting your child's development.* Washington, DC: ZERO TO THREE Press.

Miché, M. (2002). *Weaving music into young minds.* Albany, NY: Delmar.

Miller, K. (2000). *Things to do with toddlers and twos* (Revised ed.). Beltsville, MD: TelShare Publishing Co., Inc.

Neuman, S. B., & Dickinson, D. K. (Eds.). (2002). *Handbook of early literacy research.* New York, NY: The Guilford Press.

Olds, A. R. (2001). *Child care design guide.* New York, NY: McGraw-Hill.

Oser, C., & Cohen, J. (2003). *America's babies: The ZERO TO THREE Policy Center data book.* Washington, DC: ZERO TO THREE Press.

Pica, R. (2004). *Experiences in movement: Birth to age 8* (3rd ed.). Clifton Park, NY: Delmar Learning.

Raines, S., Miller, K., & Curry-Rood, L. (2002). *Story stretchers for infants, toddlers, and twos: Experiences, activities, and games for popular children's books.* Beltsville, MD: Gryphon House.

Sawyer, W. E. (2004). *Growing up with literature.* Clifton Park, NY: Delmar Learning.

Segal, M. (1998). *Your child at play: Birth to one year* (2nd ed.). New York, NY: Newmarket Press.

Shore, R. (1997). *Rethinking the brain: New insights into early development.* New York, NY: Families and Work Institute.

Torelli, L., & Durrett, C. (1998). *Landscapes for learning: Designing group care environments for infants, toddlers and two-year-olds.* Berkeley, CA: Torelli/Durrett Infant & Toddler Child Care Furniture.

U. S. Department of Health and Human Services, Administration for Children and Families, Administration on Children, Youth and Families, Head Start Bureau, Head Start Facilities. (2000). *Head Start center design guide.* Washington, DC: Author.